Isaac Preston Cory, Edward Richmond Hodges

**Cory's Ancient Fragments**

of the Phoenician, Carthaginian, Babylonian, Egyptian and other authors

Isaac Preston Cory, Edward Richmond Hodges

**Cory's Ancient Fragments**
*of the Phoenician, Carthaginian, Babylonian, Egyptian and other authors*

ISBN/EAN: 9783337239541

Printed in Europe, USA, Canada, Australia, Japan

Cover: Foto ©Andreas Hilbeck / pixelio.de

More available books at **www.hansebooks.com**

# CORY'S
# ANCIENT FRAGMENTS

OF THE

## PHŒNICIAN, CARTHAGINIAN, BABYLONIAN,

## EGYPTIAN AND OTHER AUTHORS.

---

### A New and Enlarged Edition;

THE TRANSLATION CAREFULLY REVISED, AND ENRICHED WITH NOTES
CRITICAL AND EXPLANATORY, WITH INTRODUCTIONS
TO THE SEVERAL FRAGMENTS.

---

BY

## E. RICHMOND HODGES,

M.C.P.; FELLOW OF THE SOCIETY OF BIBLICAL ARCHÆOLOGY; LATE MISSIONARY TO THE
JEWS IN EGYPT, SYRIA, AND NORTH AFRICA; EDITOR OF THE "PRINCIPIA HEBRAICA;"
AND JOINT-REVISER (WITH DR. GOTCH) OF THE "AUTHORISED VERSION OF
THE OLD TESTAMENT" FROM THE HEBREW AND CHALDEE TEXTS.

---

LONDON:
REEVES & TURNER, 196, STRAND.

1876.

TO

# SAMUEL BIRCH, LL.D.,

KEEPER OF THE ORIENTAL ANTIQUITIES IN THE BRITISH MUSEUM ;

PRESIDENT OF THE SOCIETY OF BIBLICAL ARCHÆOLOGY,

ETC., ETC., ETC.

AS A SCHOLAR TO WHOM THE NINETEENTH CENTURY IS

INDEBTED FOR THE RESUSCITATION OF SO MUCH OF

THE LONG-BURIED LEARNING OF THE ANCIENT

WORLD, THIS VOLUME IS INSCRIBED, WITH

THE MOST PROFOUND RESPECT AND

ADMIRATION, BY

THE EDITOR.

# TABLE OF CONTENTS.

*Those pieces which are for the first time published in this work are marked with a \*.*

## SANCHONIATHON.

## THE TYRIAN ANNALS.

### *From* DIUS *and* MENANDER.

## THE PERIPLUS OF HANNO.

---

## CHALDÆAN HISTORY.

*From* BEROSUS, ABYDENUS, *and* MEGASTHENES.

### CHALDÆAN FRAGMENTS.

## EGYPTIAN HISTORIES.

*Containing the* OLD CHRONICLE; *the Remains of* MANETHO; *and the* LATERCULUS *of* ERATOSTHENES.

### MISCELLANEOUS FRAGMENTS.

## INDIAN FRAGMENTS.

### From MEGASTHENES.

## ATLANTIC AND PANCHÆAN FRAGMENTS.

### From MARCELLUS and EUEMERUS.

## MISCELLANEOUS FRAGMENTS.

# ADVERTISEMENT.

THE work of which we here present to the public a new edition, was published by the late Isaac Preston Cory nearly half a century ago. After a few years a new and enlarged edition [1] was called for, which was so well received by the public that it has long been out of print. The book being still in great demand by students of antiquity, we have resolved on meeting the wishes of the public by issuing a new edition. We have caused the translation to be revised, and have added introductions to the several fragments, together with notes and explanations supplied from the recently-interpreted hieroglyphic and cuneiform texts, and from the researches of competent scholars. We have thus sought to make the student acquainted with the various sources of information which have been discovered since this collection of fragments first appeared, and to throw some light from the mounds of Nineveh and the temples of Egypt upon these relics of the long-forgotten past.

---

[1] The 2nd edition was published in 1832.

# EDITOR'S PREFACE.

In giving to the public a new edition of Cory's Ancient Fragments I have endeavoured to respond to the wishes of numerous literary friends by furnishing a brief account of the several authors to whom we are indebted for these extracts, and, at the same time, some information respecting the decipherment of the hieroglyphic texts of Egypt, and the cuneiform records of Nineveh and Babylon.

The first edition of this work appeared in 1826, the second in 1832; therefore, at a time when Egyptian scholarship was still in its infancy, while cuneiform research had not yet seen the light. The discoveries of Champollion, Young, Birch, Bunsen, Brugsch, Chabas, Le Page Renouf, Godwin, and a host of other scholars in the former field of research, and of Layard, Botta, Rawlinson, Norris, Oppert, Menant, George ·Smith, Sayce, Fox Talbot, and Schrader in the latter, have furnished so much valuable information respecting the ancient empires of Egypt and Assyria, that we can no longer rest satisfied with the meagre accounts transmitted to us by the classic writers concerning times and people with which they were themselves but imperfectly

acquainted.  At a time, therefore, when, thanks to
the labours of the distinguished scholars above
named, we can read with considerable facility and
astonishing certainty the papyri of Egypt and the
clay-tablets of Babylon, it behoves us to pause for
a moment, and consider how this wonderful mine
of ancient treasures was discovered, and the means
by which it has been worked.  Cory's Fragments
constitute a fitting supplement to the fragments
which have been exhumed from the mounds of
Nineveh, and rescued from the tombs and mummy-
pits of Egypt.  Considered in this light they will
be found to explain and complete one another ; for,
in the one we have Assyrians and Egyptians speaking for themselves each in his own tongue ; in the
other the information is supplied through a Greek
channel, and reaches us, no doubt, more or less
coloured by the media through which it has passed.
It is only when we place the two accounts side by
side that we are in a position to estimate their
respective values, and reproduce the half obliterated
lines.  "The contents of this volume," says Cory,
in his preface, "are fragments, which have been
translated from foreign languages into Greek, or
have been quoted, or transcribed, by Greeks from
foreign authors ; or, have been written in the Greek
language by foreigners who have had access to the
archives of their own countries."

By way of supplement the original editor had

added such extracts and fragments as appear to
have descended from more ancient sources, though
they are now to be found only in the works of
Greek and Latin writers. "The classical reader,"
he continues, "will find but poor amusement in
perusing a half-barbarous dialect, replete with errors
and inconsistencies;" I have, therefore, with the
two-fold object of diminishing the price and of ob-
taining space for more valuable matter, adopted
Cory's estimate of the original, and omitted the
Greek text. By this omission the value of the work
will not be diminished, the price will be consider-
ably lower, and, without increasing the size of the
book, I am able to give valuable elucidations of the
fragments from the most recent sources of information. Those who desire to consult the originals
can still do so in Bunsen's *Egypt's Place in Universal History* (vol. I., at the end), or, in Müller's
*Fragmenta Græca ;*[1] there seemed, therefore, no
reason why I should enhance the price of the book
by publishing these specimens of "a half-barbarous
dialect," or take up the reader's time with "errors
and inconsistencies." I have *generally* given Cory's
translation, seldom departing from it except where
it was manifestly wrong, ambiguous, or ill-arranged.
Sometimes, to render the book more readable, I
have thrown two sentences into one ; but in no case
have I departed from the meaning of the author.

---

[1] Didot, *Paris*, 1841.

Where the sense was obscure or incomplete, or a
name occurred under an unusual form, I have added
in the text, but *within brackets*, the word required to
complete the meaning, or the more usual name of
the person or place. The purpose for which these
fragments are here brought together is to enable the
student of antiquity to bring as it were into one
focus all the scattered rays of light, and to project
them, thus concentrated, into the dark cavern of pri-
meval history. Why then should we render the
light still more defective by retaining more of its
smoke than is unavoidable? In other words, why
retain *unexplained*, Greek forms of well-known Hebrew, Babylonian, or Egyptian names (as our trans-
lators have done in the New Testament), where we
meet with Noe for Noah, Elias for Elijah, Jesus for
Joshua, and Eliseus for the well-known Elisha? If
we were translating a German author would it, for
instance, be tolerated for a moment if we, following
our author, gave *Mailand* as the equivalent of
Milan, called Venice by its German name *Venedig*,
or spoke of Geneva as *Genf?* Whenever, therefore,
I have met with a name which has a well-established
form in our own language, I have given, together
with the Greek, the usually-accepted English equivalent, *e.g.*, Nabuchodrosorus, I have called by his
well-known name of Nebuchadnezzar; and Ithobalus
I have called, as in our version of the Bible, Ethbaal.
It is best not to assume too much knowledge on the

part of our readers; it is more prudent to err on the side of prolixity than leave them to flounder in the mire of uncertainty. Herein I am reminded of a circumstance which came under my notice some few years back. Dining with a well-known clergyman in the west of England on one of his lecture-nights, he read to me a portion of the lecture he was that night to deliver, in which the name *Brittany* occurred several times, without any indication where it was to be sought. I suggested that he should add some short parenthetical statement as to its being in France, and in what part of that country. My friend did not see the necessity of it—he was quite sure that the intelligent audience which he was about to address knew where Brittany was—in short, they would almost feel themselves insulted in being told it was in France. I told him I thought differently, and if he liked I would put it to the test immediately. Would you have the kindness to ask Miss B.—his eldest daughter, a young lady of nineteen—to step into the study and ask *her*. If she replies off-hand I will yield the point, and assume that all the people are as intelligent and well-read in geography as Miss B. The reverend gentleman called his daughter, and put the question. She appeared much perplexed, and, without attempting a reply, after five minutes' consideration withdrew covered with blushes, repeating "No! I don't pa," to the old gentleman's evident annoyance. In speaking of Brittany that

night the worthy pastor told them to "look for it in
the map of France." If, therefore, I may seem to
some critics to have spent too much time in explain-
ing what to themselves is sufficiently intelligible, I
beg they will recollect, that among my readers there
will be many to whom such matters are not so evident; and that it is for the benefit of plain English
readers that I explain what seems so very obvious
to classical scholars. In short, having set aside the
Greek text as a costly and useless encumbrance, the
book now addresses itself to the ordinary English
student, who does not happen to have enjoyed the
advantages of an early classical training. In carrying
out my plan I shall explain Hebrew, Assyrian, Greek,
Phœnician, and Egyptian words wherever they occur,
and thus endeavour to place the English reader, so
far as these Fragments are concerned, on a level
with the best Oriental scholars of our day. I have
also referred the student to authorised translations
of cuneiform and hieroglyphic texts, whenever I
thought that any additional light was thrown by
them upon the statements contained in these Fragments. Lastly, it remains only for me to say in this
place that I have omitted Cory's preface entirely, as
resting chiefly upon the long-exploded learning of
Jacob Bryant, Faber, and Parkhurst; and have dis-
pensed altogether with the Neo-Platonic forgeries
which Cory had placed at the end, bearing the titles
respectively of, Oracles of Zoroaster, the Hermetic

Creed, the Orphic, Pythagorean, and other fragments, of doubtful authenticity and of little value. We now possess, thanks to the labours of MM. Anquetil Duperron, Spiegel, and Haug, all the remains of the so-called Zend-Avesta, of which only a small portion —the Gâthas—are regarded by competent scholars as genuine. Comparing these so-called *Oracles* of Zoroaster with the genuine fragments, we have every reason to reject them as spurious. Such as they are, however, they will be found, translated into English, in Stanley's *Lives of the Philosophers*. I have preferred, therefore, in the present edition, to omit this farrago of metaphysico-philosophical nonsense, and have added several fragments of other ancient authors containing matter of greater importance.

THE EDITOR.

London, 1876.

# ORIGIN, PROGRESS, AND RESULTS

OF

# HIEROGLYPHIC AND CUNEIFORM

# DECIPHERMENT.

*Egyptian Hieroglyphics and their Decipherment.*

THE foundation of all our knowledge of the monumental and literary treasures of Ancient Egypt is based on the fortunate discovery of the famous Rosetta Stone, now treasured up in the British Museum. In 1799, we are told by Dr. Birch (*Introduction to the Study of Hieroglyphics*), M. Boussard, of the French Expedition, discovered near Rosetta, a large stone of black granite, commonly known as the Rosetta stone, or inscription, which, at the capitulation of Alexandria, was surrendered to General Hutchinson, and presented by King George III. to the British Museum.

"It contained," he continues, "a trigrammatical inscription; one in hieroglyphics, a second in the demotic or vernacular, and a third in Greek." From the Greek translation it appeared that it was a solemn decree of the united priesthood, in synod at

Memphis, in honour of Ptolemy V., who had conferred upon them certain benefits. By the successive labours of Dr. Thomas Young, Champollion, Deveria, Dr. Birch, Bunsen, Brugsch, Chabas, and other eminent scholars, the values of the hieroglyphic characters have been determined, and the two Egyptian texts translated. In 1865 a new bilingual inscription, Greek and hieroglyphic, was discovered at San, the ancient Zoan or Tanis. This new inscription has confirmed the accuracy of our previous researches, and adds a considerable amount of new information, especially as regards geographical names.[1] Egyptologists are now able to read the important historical inscriptions found at Mount Sinai and in all parts of the land of Egypt. The literature, historical, political, religious, and philosophical, of the ancient Egyptians[2] is now spread open before us, and reflects a brilliant light upon the ancient fragments of Manetho and other writers contained in this work.

---

[1] The native name of Phœnicia, so long an insuperable difficulty to scholars, appears from this Egyptian text to have been KEFT—*i.e.*, a palm-tree. See the Hebrew text of Isaiah ix. 13, xix. 15, and Job xv. 32.

[2] The most important Egyptian texts, translated by competent scholars, are now accessible to English readers in vols II., IV., and VI. of *Records of the Past*. Bagster & Sons, London, 1873—5.

## Cuneiform Decipherment.

DURING the past quarter of a century a new and unexpected revelation has come to us from the plains of Mesopotamia and the banks of the Tigris. The buried cities of Babylon and Nineveh, of Erech, and Arbela, have sprung from their long-forgotten graves, and yielded to Botta and Layard, Rawlinson and Loftus, their ancient records and historic treasures. In our early days Nineveh was but a name, and Babylon an abstraction : their annals were partially recorded in the venerable pages of Holy Writ, and we had glimpses of their ancient glories in the histories and poems of the classic writers ; but their sites were unknown, or unidentified, and the wandering Arab or Eeliyaut pitched his tent and tended his flocks among their long-forgotten sepulchres.

Still, amidst all this ruin and obscurity there existed a key to unlock the treasures of the past : the man only was wanted who should discover and employ it. We purpose, therefore, on the present occasion to answer the oft-repeated question, How have we attained the power to read and translate the cuneiform inscriptions of the Assyrians and Babylonians, and what proof can be given of our success therein ?

The collections of Europe, but, more especially those of the Louvre and the British Museum, contain innumerable specimens of Assyrian sculpture, and whole volumes of Assyrian history — history, as has been well observed, written " not in books, nor on paper, but upon rocks and stones " — cylinders of baked clay and burnt bricks. It is, we believe, generally known that these inscriptions, so far as they relate historical matter, can now be read and translated with almost as much ease, and with nearly the same accuracy, as a page of Sanskrit or Arabic ; but few, we believe, are acquainted with the process by which this power has been attained. The readers of the Journal of the Royal Asiatic Society are no doubt aware of the painful steps by which this success has been achieved ; but the great majority of intellectual people—not being members of that learned Society —are in the deepest ignorance with reference to this interesting question. Rarely have we met with any one who had clear and accurate knowledge of the origin of cuneiform decipherment, and of the vast importance of the results attained. Though always taking a deep interest in such discoveries ourselves, we confess that, if any one had asked us five or six years ago what we knew of the subject, we should have been compelled in truth to say, Very little ! Our first accurate and connected ideas upon the subject were derived from the very valuable work of M. Menant, " *Les Écritures Cunéiformes, Exposé des travaux qui ont preparé la lecture et l'interpretation des inscriptions de la Perse et de l'Assyrie,*" 2nd edition, Paris, 1864.

When Botta and Layard excavated the mounds of
Mesopotamia, and brought to light their buried
treasures to adorn our museums, and throw a gleam
of light on the sadly blurred and blotted pages of
antiquity, the nature of the cuneiform characters was
comparatively unknown. From the days of the British
Resident at Bagdad, Mr. Rich, and Sir Robert Ker
Porter, inscriptions in the cuneiform character were
continually being published and conjecturally interpreted by charlatans and pretenders; but no real
basis was found on which to rear the vast fabric
which was destined to be built. Grotefend, of
Göttingen, in the beginning of the present century,
was the first to lay the foundation-stone of cuneiform
decipherment. Münter and Tychsen had previously
identified the group for " king," and established the
use of the diagonally-placed wedge as a word-divider.

A copy of two short inscriptions found at Persepolis,
was placed before Grotefend, the one of Darius Hystaspes, the other of his son Xerxes. He conjectured
that, probably, these were inscriptions emanating
from a Persian monarch of the Achæmenide dynasty,
or successors of Achæmenes ; he fixed upon a
certain group of characters, which, from their frequent recurrence, might contain the name of some
king of that dynasty. Taking one of these short inscriptions, he tried the names of Xerxes and of Cyrus,
but without success. He then tried that of Darius,
and succeeded. By the decipherment of this name

he obtained the values of five or six cuneiform
characters : he read the name Dara-ya-vush or Darius,
and his title *khshayathiya khshayathiyânam,* "king of
kings, son of Vistaspa," &c., which furnished several
more phonetic values. Distinguished scholars, such
as Westergard, and Rask, of Copenhagen, Lassen,
of Bonn, and Burnouf, of Paris, then took up the
study on the Continent, while Dr. Hincks and Mr.
Fox Talbot devoted their attention to the decipherment of the third kind of inscriptions, the Assyrian.
Our Universities have produced as yet no cuneiform
scholars, with the exception of Hincks and Sayce,
nor can we point out any distinguished clergyman in
the Church, except Mr. Sayce,[1] who has devoted
himself to this study. Yet, in spite of much in-
difference, and not a little determined opposition,
progress continued to be made. Hitherto only copies
of the two short inscriptions found at Persepolis, the
one a decree of Xerxes, the other of Darius, had
formed the sole materials for study. A longer text
was then found on the rocks of Elvend, which soon
attracted the attention of the savants of Europe.
Burnouf devoted himself to the study of the Persian
text, and De Saulcy to the Assyrian. Fortunately,
all these inscriptions emanating from the Persian
monarchs, are drawn up in *three* languages, and it is

---

[1] Since this was written the Rev. J. M. Rodwell has
translated from the cuneiform text the Annals of Asur-
nasir-pal, king of Assyria, B.C. 883.

by their aid that we have been able to overcome
the difficulties, otherwise insuperable, of reading the
annals of Assyrian and Babylonian kings. The
brevity of all the trilingual inscriptions hitherto
known in Europe, however, limited our knowledge
to but a few cuneiform characters, and to still fewer
words. The long-desired key was at length found
in the very long inscription of Darius Hystaspes at
Behistun, in Persia.[1] We owe the first copy of this
very valuable document to Sir Henry Rawlinson,
who, while engaged in official duties as H. M.
ambassador to the Court of Persia, embraced the
opportunity afforded him by its proximity to Ker-
manshah to procure a copy of it. The Persian text
he published with a Latin translation in the Journal
of the Royal Asiatic Society for 1846, and the
Assyrian text, with a translation into Latin, in the
same Journal in 1851.

Here the scholars of Europe had a text on which
to exercise their ingenuity, and one worthy of their
exertions. The Persian text is written with a
cuneiform alphabet of about 40 characters; the
Medo-Scythic and the Assyrian translations of the
text are written, the former with a syllabarium, and
the latter in ideograms, and with a syllabarium. This
inscription, which for ages had attracted the attention of travellers going into Media, was ascribed in

---

[1] See the article, *Behistun Inscription*, in the *English
Cyclopædia*, Supplement, *Arts and Sciences*.

the time of Diodorus Siculus to the celebrated queen
Semiramis.  Instead of this, we know now that it is a
record of the acts and conquests of Darius Hystaspes,
who there gives his genealogy, and mentions the
various battles fought by him against the successive
pretenders to the throne.  The tone of piety in which
it is written, the religious feeling shown throughout
in the ascription of all his victories to Ormuzd, the
supreme deity of the Persians, and the love of truth
there inculcated, render this a very valuable testimony to the state of religious and moral feeling at
that remote period.  The names and facts recorded,
also, most surprisingly confirm the statements of the
Greek authors, Herodotus and Diodorus.

Interesting as the Behistun Inscription undoubtedly
is, it becomes still more so as being the starting-point
of Babylonian and Assyrian decipherment.  There
are more than ninety proper-names in the Assyrian
text of this inscription ;  and, since proper-names are
not *translated*, but only *transcribed* from one language
into another, it follows, that having by the decom-
position of these ninety names, obtained a portion
of the Assyrian syllabary, we were *then* in a position
to commence the reading of the remainder of the
inscription.  The Persian text of the Behistun
Inscription was our first spelling-book, and its
renderings our first dictionary of the Assyrio-Babylonian language.  But, it may be asked, How did we
obtain a key to the Persian text ?  It is true that

Grotefend, Burnouf, Lassen, Oppert, and Hincks
had laboured with Sir H. Rawlinson at the discovery
of the phonetic values of the Persian characters ; but
who gave us the vocabulary ?  This also was a work
of time ; but the publication of the Zend-Avesta by
Anquetil-Duperron, the study of the Zend, or Old
Bactrian, and Sanskrit languages, all contributed to
aid the student in determining the meaning of the
Persian words.   In fact, many of the words are
identical with the Sanskrit, *e.g.*, putra—a son ; bratar
—a brother ; bhumi—earth ; bâga—a god ; bu—to
be, to exist ; nâvi—a ship ; and many others, are
all unchanged Sanskrit words, while *âdam* is only a
harder form of the Sanskrit *aham*—I. .

Then, again, the modern Persian was of great assistance.   Darius commences his address with " I am
Darius, the great king, king of kings," &c.   Now
such words as *khshâyathiya* and *vazraka* were easily
explained from the corresponding Persian words
shah—a king, buzurg—great; and so of a great
many others.

The labours of Sir Henry Rawlinson have been
carried on and perfected by Spiegel, an eminent
German savant, and now we find there are not twenty
words in the whole Persian text of the meaning
of which there is any doubt.   The Assyrio-Babylonian inscription is a tolerably correct translation of
the Persian text.   Having, therefore, obtained the
values of the Assyrian characters by pulling to pieces,

as it were, the ninety proper-names occurring in the Assyrian translation, we were able, by the help of the Persian translation, to render, word for word, the meaning of the Assyrio-Babylonian text.    Dr. Hincks afterwards compiled a syllabary, as did also Sir H. Rawlinson, and Dr. Oppert.

An attempt was now made at translating for the first time a uni-lingual text—the Standard inscription of Sargon from Khorsabad.    This was translated by Major-General Sir Henry Rawlinson, and published in the Journal of the Royal Asiatic Society for 1850.    At the same time, Sir Henry also published, in the same Journal, a translation of the inscription on the famous Black Obelisk, recording the events of the reign of Shalmaneser II., King of Assyria.    This venerable monument was brought by Mr. Layard from Nimroud, the ancient Calakh, and is now in the British Museum.    The text of these two inscriptions, with many others of even greater antiquity, has been published by command of the Trustees of the British Museum.

The learned world still remained incredulous as to the accuracy of what had been done, and still, though without any sufficient reason, a few persons remain so.    Professor E. Renan, and some other eminent scholars, impugned the accuracy of the translations, but it arose from their ignorance of the subject, and from their unwillingness to climb the tedious ascent which all who pursue cuneiform studies must ascend.

The translation of the first four years of the annals of Tiglath-Pileser Ist (B. C. 1100) (not the one mentioned in the Bible), by the four most eminent cuneiform scholars of that day, published in extenso in the Journal of the Royal Asiatic Society for 1860, formed a new era in cuneiform scholarship. Sir Henry Rawlinson, Mr. Fox Talbot, Dr. Edward Hincks, and Dr. Oppert, of Paris, laboured severally on this inscription. Their independent translations are printed side by side, and any impartial critic may see plainly that on the whole there is a very remarkable coincidence in their renderings. To use the words of the arbitrators, " That they are all agreed, or very nearly so, as to the powers of the characters, is established by their concurrent readings of proper names, which they almost always express in as nearly the same manner as can be expected, when we consider the different values attached by different persons to the letters of our own alphabet." Again, they say, " The agreement as regards the letters being established, it follows that significant terms will be also similarly read ; and this may be assumed to be the case from the frequent correspondence in the passages of the translations. It may be stated generally, that with a few exceptions, the main purport of each paragraph agrees." They conclude their judgment on the several translations as follows :—" Upon the whole, the result of this experiment—than which a fairer test could scarcely be devised — may be considered as establishing, almost definitely, the correctness of the valuation of the *characters* of these inscriptions. It is possible that further investigations may find something to alter, or to add ; but, the great portion, if not the whole, may be read with confidence." One would have thought that after such a decided expression of opinion by the most competent scholars, who consented to act as arbitrators, that the cavillers would have been for ever silenced. But it is not so : there are still a few who are utterly incredulous as to the certainty, or accuracy, of cuneiform scholarship. Fifteen years have elapsed since then, and our cuneiform scholars have not been idle : Dr. Oppert visited the ruins of Nineveh and Babylon, and on his return published, at the cost of the French Government, his excellent and learned work, "*Expedition en Mesopotamie,*" which contains numerous texts, with translations and vocabularies of words. The same author has given us the Annals of Sargon (mentioned Isaiah xx.), an Early History of Babylon and Assyria, and to him belongs the merit of first publishing an Assyrian Grammar. Dr. Edwin Norris, late secretary of the Royal Asiatic Society, has given to the world a translation of the *Medo-Scythic* text of the Behistun Inscription ; and, till his decease, was employed on his invaluable *Assyrian Dictionary*, three volumes of which have long been in the hands of cuneiform scholars. Monsieur Joachim Ménant has favoured the public with a valuable grammar of the Assyrian language in the cuneiform character; Mr. Fox Talbot has introduced many admirable translations of cuneiform inscriptions, and is now engaged in the preparation of a very useful Glossary of Assyrio-Babylonian words; while Mr. George Smith, of the British Museum, is deserving of all praise for his very valuable work, entitled the "*Annals of Asurbanipal, son of Esarhaddon, king of Assyria,*" with text and translation; his complete List of Assyrian Characters and Ideograms; and lastly, for his admirable sketch of *Early Babylonian History,* published in the first vol. of the Transactions of the Society of Biblical Archaeolgy, and reprinted, with additions, in vol. iii. of *Records of the Past.* So far we have traced the origin and progress of cuneiform decipherment. We have now briefly to speak of the results attained, or yet to be obtained, by the pursuit of this study.

First. We have established the important fact that the Assyrians were a Semitic people, and spoke a language akin to Hebrew and Arabic.

Secondly. We learn of the existence, in prehistoric times, of a great Turanian civilisation in the plains of Mesopotamia. We learn the surprising fact that, at a remote period, a people allied to the Finns and Laplanders, and speaking a dialect of the great Tartar family, founded the cities of central Asia, invented the most complex system of writing that human ingenuity ever devised, and laid the foundation of a civilisation which lasted with few radical changes down to the time of Alexander the Great. Some of their cities are mentioned in Holy Scripture, as Erech and Accad in the land of Shinar; and this primitive people is often mentioned in the inscriptions of the Assyrian kings, and called *Akkadi*, or Akkads.[1] We possess numerous specimens of their literature in the British Museum, and we find that they were a highly civilized race, who have left us historical annals, scientific treatises, liturgies, and mythological tracts. Their language not only permeated the Assyrian, but even reached the Hebrew, in which are found several Akkad words, such as yam—sea, hékal— a temple, ír—a city, and many others. The Akkads were the instructors of the Assyrians in literature and science, and from them the Assyrians adopted the arrow-headed, or wedge-shaped system of writing, which we call cuneiform.

Thirdly. We have learned by the decipherment of the Assyrian inscriptions, the origin of that remarkable Hebrew word עַשְׁתֵּי (ASHTÉ), which has been the crux of Hebrew scholars. Joined to the word עָשָׂר it denotes eleven. Winer, an eminent Hebrew scholar, thought that "having counted ten

---

[1] See the article *Chaldee Language*, in the *English Cyclopædia*, Supplement, *Arts and Sciences;* also, M. François Lenormant's learned work, *Etudes Acadiennes*, Paris, 1873.

upon their fingers, ash-tay-âsâr must mean something kept in mind over and above the ten, and hence
eleven." Gesenius, the prince of Hebrew scholars,
commenting on this conjecture of Winer's, cries out
in despair, "By Hercules it is not probable, but
I can offer nothing more satisfactory." Had Gesenius
lived to our times he would have recognised this
strange word in the Assyrian *ishtin*—one; the
Hebrew, Arabic, and Syriac being respectively
*akhad, wahaad,* and *ekhdo.*

Fourthly. We read in the annals of the Assyrian
kings of their wars and conquests—what countries
they subdued, what peoples they carried away
into captivity, and with what kings they made cove-
nants and alliance. To every lover of the Bible
it must be a source of great satisfaction to find
mention made in the Assyrian inscriptions of Tyre
and Sidon, and Jerusalem and Gaza, and Samaria
(sometimes called Omri). And not only names of
Biblical *places,* but of Biblical *persons* are to be
found there; as Hezekiah and Jehoahaz, Ahab
and Jehu, and Hazael, Sennacherib, Esarhaddon,
and Nebuchadnezzar. Under this head of scriptural illustration will come the deeply interesting
fact, that we now obtain evidence of the true pronunciation of the sacred and incommunicable name
of God. It is, we believe, generally admitted
among Hebrew scholars, that the name *Jehovah,* as
the designation of the supreme God, is incorrect.

The Jews never pronounce this name.[1] You never meet with it in the New Testament; showing that even at that time either the true pronunciation was *lost*, or it was considered unlawful to pronounce it, which is the statement of Philo Judæus, confirmed by Josephus. Some Hebraists contend for *Yahveh* as the correct pronunciation, but with little proof. We learn, however, from an Assyrian inscription of Sargon's that the correct pronunciation of the most sacred name of God amongst the Semitic people was Ya-u, or Yâhū. In the Cyprus Inscription of Sargon we read of a certain Ya-hu-bîdi, king of Hamath. Now as this king's name is preceded by the sign indicating a god, it is evident that his name is a compound of some divine name, such as Yahu's servant, in which it resembles the Hebrew name Jehoahaz, more correctly Yeho-ahaz—" one who holds to Yeho," or Jehovah. In the book of Psalms, too, we are told to praise God by his name Yah, which is an abbreviated form of Yahu.

Lastly. That this was the most sacred name of God as taught in the mysteries we learn from Macrobius and Plutarch. We may assume, therefore, from the very accurate mode of Assyrian vocalization, that we have here the correct pronunciation of a Semitic

---

[1] See on this point the excellent observations of Dr. Ginsburg, in pp. 22 and 23 of *The Moabite Stone*, 4to, Reeves & Turner, 2nd edition, 1871.

name as found in an Assyrian inscription, and that
Ya-hu, or *Ya-ho*, and not Jehovah, is the correct
pronunciation of what has been called " the ineffable
name" of the Most High.

Time would fail to point out the many points of
interest of a historical, philological, and chronological character upon which Assyrian literature
throws a flood of light. We are yet upon the
threshold of the temple of truth; we have not
penetrated into its adytum. The library of Ashur-
banipal is not yet all published, and there are
doubtless thousands of deeply interesting inscriptions
of great antiquity still lying buried under the mounds
of Mesopotamia. These have yet to be exhumed
and brought to light, and we trust that our Government will resume the excavations of Botta and
Layard, send out competent scholars[1] to explore
the ancient ruins, copy and translate inscriptions,
and rescue from oblivion the stores of valuable
information contained there. We have many inscriptions of Nebuchadnezzar's, but all we possess,
at present, merely refer to his restorations and
improvements of the city of Babylon. We want the
account of his conquests, particularly that of his

---

[1] The proprietors of the *Daily Telegraph*, with great
public spirit, have since commissioned Mr. George Smith
to go to Assyria. Mr. Smith has subsequently undertaken
further researches (in a second journey) at Mosul, for the
Trustees of the British Museum.

capture of Jerusalem, and transportation of the Jews,
and there is no doubt that such inscriptions exist,
and, with many similar records of other kings, are
worthy of our earnest search.    Let not those relics
of a past age lie mouldering in their graves.    Let
England's sons, who prize and love the Bible, exert
themselves, and show a deep and sincere interest in
excavations and discoveries which  throw light on its
sacred pages, and confirm its hallowed truths.

# SANCHONIATHON.

PHŒNICIAN literature has perished, leaving barely the traces of its former existence. That the Phœnicians, however, at a very early period were a literary people, who spoke a language almost identical with the Hebrew[1] we have Biblical evidence, even if it rested on the single fact, that the city subsequently called Debir, was originally called, during the Canaanite or Phœnician occupation, before Joshua's conquest of the land, by the name of Kiryath-Sepher, or Book-town. We know also, from other sources, that Phœnician merchants were often philosophers, Carthaginian generals, and states-men, literary men, and that Numidian kings, who had received a Phœnician education and training, possessed libraries of Phœnician works ; or, as Juba and Hiempsal, were themselves authors.

The Phœnicians, like most Semitic nations,—the Jews for instance—had a very ancient historical

---

[1] See the Article *Phœnician Language and Inscriptions*, in the *English Cyclopædia* (Arts and Sciences Supplement).

literature, no doubt originating with the inscriptions, which, in order to perpetuate the memory of past events were preserved in their temples, and when the Semitic world became better known to the Greeks, historical works of Phœnician origin are mentioned in a general way, and, in some cases, the supposed authors of them are designated. Among them we meet with three names, Mochus, Hypsikrates, and Theodotus, whose works are said to have been by one Chaitus translated into Greek. The work of Mochus, of which several Greek editions existed, began with the Cosmogony, and after the time of Eudemus is often quoted.   Of the other two, little is known except that Hypsikrates is supposed by some to be the same as our author Sanchoniathon ; an hypothesis grounded upon the circumstance that Hypsikrates in Greek signifies the same as Sanchoniathon in Phœnician, which Movers interprets סֵם מִכְנָתוֹ, SAM-ME-KUNATHO = *the height* (*i.e.*, heaven) *is his throne*.   In the same manner, *Theodotus* may be the Greek rendering of the common Phœnician name בַּעְלִיתֶּן, BAAL-YITTEN, *i.e.*, *Baal gives*.   Numerous Greek *réchauffés* of historical works, originally composed in the Phœnician language, are also known to us, bearing the names of Asclepiades, Chaitus, Claudius, Julius, Dius, Hieronymus the Egyptian, Histiaeus, Menander of Pergamus, Menander of Ephesus, Philistus, Posidonius, Philostratus, and Teucer of Cyzicus ; while we have it on record, that Hiempsal, King of Numidia, wrote a history of Libya, which is quoted by Sallust. Mago, the famous Carthaginian general, wrote twenty-eight books on agriculture, which Dionysius of Utica rendered into Greek, and Silanus, by command of the Roman senate, translated into Latin. As regards Sanchoniathon, the author of the following fragments, almost nothing is known. He is mentioned by Athenaeus (lib. iii. cap. 37), Porphyry, the great opponent of Christianity (*De Abstinentia*, lib. ii. sec. 56), Theodoret (*De Cur. Græc. Affect.*, serm. ii.), by Suidas, who calls him a " Tyrian philosopher ;" and, by Eusebius (*De Præparatione Evangelica*, lib. ii. c. 11). For the fragments of his work which have escaped the shipwreck of time, we are principally indebted to Eusebius and his opponent Porphyry. All has perished except those quotations, made for polemical purposes, by the writers above named. From their pages they have been again extracted, put together, and are here placed before 'the reader for his examination. Owing to the entire loss of Sanchoniathon's original, we are indebted for what we know of his work to a translation into Greek made by a certain Philo (B.C. 100) of Byblus, a coast town of Phœnicia.[1] But we must not withhold from our readers that the

---

[1] Byblus, the Gebal of the Hebrew Scriptures, is the present Jebail, situated on the sea coast between Beyrout and Tripoli.

loss of the original, together with the fragmentary
character of what remains to us of Philo's translation,
diminish not a little from its value. Hence many
have denied the genuineness of these fragments altogether, among whom we may mention Ursinus,
Dodwell, Van Dale, Meiners, Hissman, and Lobeck.
Others, as Grotius, Goguet, Mignot, Ewald, and the
late Baron Bunsen, have considered these fragments
as genuine, and regard the substance of them as
really Phœnician, and therefore of the highest importance. Those who desire to see what has been
advanced in their favour may consult with advantage
the Introduction to Goguet's *Esprit de Lois*, Spiegel's
article, " Sanchoniathon," in Hertzog's *Real Encyclo-
pädie*, and especially an able article by Prof. Renan,
*on the Sources of Sanchoniathon's history*, entitled
" *Mémoire sur l'origine et le charactère veritable de
l'histoire Phœnicienne qui porte le nom de Sanchoniathon*," in the " *Mémoires de l'Académie des Inscriptions*," Paris, 1860.[1] Having thus pointed out the
sources of further information regarding the work of
Sanchoniathon, and its historical value, we consider
our task will be completed by presenting the fragments to the reader, with such elucidations of the

---

[1] On the opposite side the reader may consult with ad-
vantage Mover's, *Die Unechtheit der in Eusebius erhaltenen
Fragmente des Sanchoniathon bewiesen. Jahrbuch für Kath.
Theologie.*

Phœnician and Greek words as occur therein ; and then, leaving the student to form his own judgment, as to their genuineness and importance. Volumes might be written on either side ; and, knowing the weight of argument to be pretty evenly balanced, we prefer to take no side, but allow the student, un-biassed by any opinion of our own, to judge for himself.

# SANCHONIATHON.

"Now these things a certain Sanchoniathon has
handed down to posterity, a very ancient author
whom they testify flourished before the Trojan war,
and who, commended both for his industry and fidelity, wrote the History of the Phœnicians. All the
writings of this author, Philo, not the Jew of that
name, but of Byblus, having translated out of the
Phœnician, published in the Greek language.

He supposes that the beginning of all things was
a dark and condensed windy air, or a breeze of dark

---

[1] Eusebius (surnamed Pamphilus), born A.D. 264, was a
native of Palestine. Being elevated to the see of Cæsarea,
he died about 338. He was a voluminous writer, and among
his other works he composed the *Præparatio Evangelica*, in
nine volumes, which he dedicated to Theodotus, Bishop of
Laodicea. This famous work, upon which his renown
chiefly rests, contains fragments of Sanchoniathon, Berosus,
and others whose works have since entirely perished.

B

air, and a chaos turbid and black as Erebus ;[1] and
that these were unbounded, and for a long series of
ages destitute of form [or limit].[2]  But when this wind
became enamoured of its own first principles (the
chaos), and an intimate union took place, that con-
nexion was called Pothos ;[3] and it was the beginning of the creation of all things.  And it (the Chaos)
knew not its own production ; but, from its embrace[4]
with the wind, was generated Môt, which some called
Ilus (mud) ; but others the putrefaction of a watery
mixture.  And from this sprung all the seed of the
creation, and the generation of the universe.  And
there were certain animals, not having sensation,
from which intelligent animals were produced ;
and they were called Zophasemim, [צוֹפֵי הַשָּׁמַיִם,

---

[1]   "From Chaos Erebus and ebon Night :
      From Night the Day sprang forth, and shining air,
      Whom to the love of Erebus she gave."
                    *Hesiod's Theogony* (Elton's Translation), line 170.

[2] Gen. i. 2, where עֶרֶב ('EREV), denotes *mixture, twilight,*
and hence *evening.* · "The earth was without form, and
void."—Gen. i. 1.

[3] Pothos or Desire. *This seems to be the same as* Ερως, *or
Cupid, who was held by the Greek mythologists to be the prime
cause of all things.*—See Hesiod's Theogony, v. 120, and
Wolff's note upon it.

[4] This union was symbolized among the heathen, and
particularly by the Phœnicians, by an egg enfolded by a
serpent, which *disjunctively* represented the Chaos and the
Æther ; but, when *united* the hermaphroditic first principle
of the universe, *i.e.* Cupid, or Pothos.

Tsophe hashshamayim], *i.e.*, *observers of heaven*, and they were formed similar to the shape of an egg. And Môt shone out with the sun, and the moon, and the less and the greater stars. "*Such* (adds Eusebius), "*is their Cosmogony, directly bringing in Atheism. But let us see in continuation how he states the origin of the animal creation. He says then,* ' And when the air began to send forth light, by its fiery influence on the sea and earth, winds were produced, and clouds, and very great defluxions and outpourings of the heavenly waters. And after that these things were divided and separated from their proper place by the heat of the sun, and then all met again in the air, and dashed together, whence thunders and lightnings were formed ; and at the crash of those thunders the above-named intelligent animals were awakened and frightened with the sound ; and then male and female moved on the earth and in the sea. *This* (says Eusebius) *is their generation of animals. After this our author* (Sanchoniathon) *proceeds to say*, ' These things are written in the Cosmogony of Taautus (Thoth),[1] and in his memoirs, and from the

---

[1] THOTH was an Egyptian deity of the second order, whose attributes are not well known. The Græco-Roman mythology identified him with Hermes, or Mercury. His sign is the Ibis, and he is the most important, according to Bunsen, of all the Cabiri. He was reputed to be the inventor of writing, the patron deity of learning, the scribe of the gods, in which capacity he is represented signing the sentences on the souls of the dead.

conjectures and evidences which his mind saw and
found out, and wherewith he hath enlightened us.
*Afterwards* (says Eusebius) *declaring the names of
the winds, Notus, Boreas and the rest, he makes this
epilogue:* ' But these first men consecrated the pro-
ductions of the earth, and judged them gods, and
worshipped those things upon which they themselves
lived, and all their posterity and all before them : to
these they made libations (or drink-offerings), and
sacrifices.' *Then he proceeds,* 'These were the devices
of worship suited to the weakness and want of bold-
ness of their minds (*or* narrowness of their souls).—
Euseb. *Præp. Evan.,* lib. i. cap. 10.

*Then he says,* ' Of the wind Kolpia¹ and of his wife,
Baau, which is interpreted Night, were begotten two
mortal men, Aeon³ and Protogonus so called, and
Aeon discovered food from trees.   Those begotten
from these were called Genos and Genea, and inhabited Phœnicia, and when great droughts came (*upon*

---

¹ Hebrew קוֹל פִּי יָה, Kol-pi-YAH, *i.e.,* the voice of the
mouth of Yah, or Jehovah.

² Orelli, the latest editor of these fragments, thinks we
should read BAAUT, and that the τ has been omitted by
error of the copyists.   BAAUT, he thinks, might be the
Phœnician word for *night,* since in Chaldee בּוּת (BOOTH),
means *to pass the night,* as in Dan. vi. 19. (v. 18 Eng. Ver.)

³ Aeon is taken by Orelli for Eve.   Heb. חַוָּה (KHAVAH);
and Protogonus (first-born) for Adam ; while GENOS he
supposes to be Cain, and Genea his wife.

*the land*) they stretched forth their hands to heaven, towards the Sun, for this (he says), they supposed to be the only God, the Lord of Heaven, calling him BEELSAMIN, which name among the Phœnicians signifies Lord of Heaven, but among the Greeks *is equivalent* to Zeus, or Jupiter.

*After these things he charges the Greeks with error, saying,* ' For we (*the Phœnicians*), not vainly, have frequently distinguished those *names,* but with respect to the later signification of names accruing to them from later things, the Greeks, not knowing, have construed .otherwise, being led astray by the ambiguity of their signification. *Then he proceeds,* ' By Genos[1] the son of Aeon and Protogonos were again begotten mortal children, whose names were Phos, Pur, and Phlox (*i.e.* Light, Fire, and Flame). These found out the method of generating fire by rubbing together pieces of wood, and taught men the use of it (*i.e., fire*). These begat sons of vast bulk and height, whose names were given to the mountains which they occupied. Thus, from them were called Mount Cassius, and Libanus, and Antilibanus, and Brathu.[2] ' Of these men, *he says,* were begotten

---

[1] *i.e.*, Cain, as Orelli supposes. His reading is, " From the race of Aeon," &c.

[2] Orelli says he has sought in vain for this mountain in the ancient geographers ; but thinks it may have been the name of some mountain in Syria, or Arabia Deserta, where was a city mentioned by Ptolemy under the name of Berathena.

(*through intercourse*), *with* their mothers, Memrumus and Hypsuranius;[1] the women of those times without shame having intercourse with any man they might chance to meet.[2]   Then, *says he*, Hypsuranius dwelt in Tyre, and he invented huts constructed of reeds and rushes, and (*found out the use of*) papyrus. And he fell into enmity with his brother Usous, who first invented a covering for the body, of the skins of the wild beasts which he could catch.[3]   And, when violent tempests of winds and rains came, the boughs of the trees in Tyre being rubbed against each other took fire, and burnt the wood there.   And Usous having taken a tree, and lopped off its boughs, was the first man who dared to venture upon it on the

----

[1] These two names Bochart takes to be the designation of one person.  Scaliger agrees with him, taking Mem-roumous to be from מִמְּרוֹמִים, MIMMEROMIM ; whence, says Orelli, "the word Ὑψουρανιος, Hypsoranius, is only the Greek rendering of these two Phœnician words."

[2] "Who does not recognise," says Orelli in his note on this passage, "in these words the Mosaic tradition about the Nephilim (or giants), begotten from the intercourse of the sons of God with the daughters of men?"—See Genesis vi. 1, 2.

[3] Scaliger supposed here some reference to the hairy Esau.  Orelli, following Bishop Cumberland, thinks that such a reference is quite inadmissible, and that we should rather understand some antediluvian descendant of Cain, named Uz, who gave his name to a part of Syria.—See Genesis x. 23.

sea. And he consecrated two stelæ, or pillars, to Fire and Wind ;[1] and he worshipped them, and poured out to them[2] the blood of those wild beasts he had taken in the chase. And when all these men were dead, those that remained consecrated to them staves of wood, and worshipped stelæ, or pillars, and celebrated feasts in honour of them every year. And in times long after these, were born of the race of Hypsuranius,[3] Agreus and Halieus (*i.e.* Hunter and Fisherman), the inventors of the arts of hunting and fishing, from whom hunters and fishermen are named.[4] Of these were begotten two brothers, the inventors of iron and the manifold uses of it. One of these, called Chrysor (whom he says is Vulcan), exercised

---

[1] The atmosphere and winds, we are told by Julius Firmicus, received divine honours from the Assyrians and people on the shores of Africa, while fire was equally venerated in all the colonies of the Phœnicians, especially in the temple of the Tyrian Hercules at Cadiz (Gades), to extinguish the perpetual fire in which was punished with death.—See Creuzer's *Symbolik* and Münter, *Religion der Karthager*, 49, 61. Orelli's note, *in loc.*

[2] *i.e.*, the pillars, as representing the mysterious agency of wind and fire.

[3] *i.e.*, 'Elion, or the Most High.

[4] On this passage Orelli says : "These are Greek renderings of Syrophœnician names. In Hebrew it would read thus : 'And 'Elion begat Said and Sidon, whence the Sidones and Sidonians are named ;' for צוּד (Tsood) means both *to hunt* and *to fish.*"

himself in words and charms, and divinations ; and he invented the hook, bait, and fishing-line, and coracles, or light fishing boats ; and he was the first of men who sailed (*i.e., who applied sails to the propelling of ships*). Wherefore men worshipped him after his death as a God, and they called him Diamichius,[1] i.e., *the great inventor;* and some say his brothers invented the making of walls with bricks. After these things, of his race were born two young men, one of whom was called Technites, *i.e.,* the Artist ; the other, Geinos Autochthon,[2] i.e. *earthborn,* or generated from the earth itself. These men found out how to mix stubble with the brick-earth, and to dry the *bricks so made* in the sun : they were also the inventors of tiling. By these were begotten others, of whom one was called Agrus (Field), the

---

[1] This, as Cumberland remarks, is the first instance of deification. To Chrysor, says Orelli, "the Phœnicians seem to have attributed all those arts which the Greeks referred to the three gods, Vulcan, Mercury, and Apollo. Chrysor may be, as Cumberland supposed, from the Hebrew חָרַץ (KHARATS), which has the meaning of *sharpening, cutting, etc.* In Assyrian it means *gold.*

[2] As Adam may have been designated before by the name of Protogonus, so here, under the name of Geinos Autochthon, Orelli supposes to be meant the first man who settled down and lived in a house constructed of sun-dried bricks, in contrast with the nomades and dwellers in huts built of rushes and reeds.

other Agroueros, or Agrotes[1] (*Husbandman*), who had a wooden statue that was much venerated, and a shrine (or portable temple),[2] drawn about in Phœnicia by yokes of oxen. And in books (*or*, at Byblus), he is called distinctly *The greatest of the Gods.* These added to the houses courts, and porticos, and crypts. Husbandmen, and such as hunt with dogs, derive their origin from these ; they are called also Aletæ, and Titans. From these were descended Amynus and Magus, who taught men to construct villages and tend flocks. By these men were begotten Misor and Sydyk, that is, *Wellfreed* and *Just :* and they found out the use of salt. From Misor[3] descended Taautus, who invented the writing of the first letters : the Egyptians called him Thoor, the Alexandrians

---

[1] Philo is here quite in error, says Scaliger, for instead of שָׂדֶה, SADEH, *a field,* he should have read *Shaddai,* שַׁדָּי, Almighty. Philo, or rather Sanchoniathon, is speaking of gods like Pan, Pales, or Sylvanus, agricultural and pastoral deities ; but he confounds one of them with the *greatest god* of the people of Byblos, the Shaddai of the Jews.

[2] Like the ark of the covenant among the Jews.—See 2 Samuel vi. 3, and compare with Amos v. 26 and Acts vii. 43.

[3] Misor, no doubt, indicates the establisher of Government in Egypt, for Mitzraim (in which name we recognise the Hebrew dual number for the Upper and Lower country) is the usual word for Egypt in the Hebrew Scriptures ; still called MISR in Arabic.

Thoyth, and the Greeks Hermes.   But from Sydyk[1]
descended the Dioscuri or Cabiri, or Corybantes, or
Samothracian deities.   These (*he says*), first invented
a ship.   From these descended others who were the
discoverers of medicinal herbs, and of the cure of
poisons, and of charms.   Contemporary with these
was one Elioun,[2] called Hypsistus (*i.e. the most high*) ;
and his wife named Beruth,[3] and they dwelt about
Byblus [*the Hebrew* Gebal].   By these was begotten
Epigeus, or Autochthon, whom they afterwards called
Ouranos (*i.e.* Heaven) ; so that from him that element which is over us, by reason of its excellent
beauty, is named heaven.   And he had a sister of
the same parents, and she was called Gē (*i.e.*, Earth),
and by reason of her beauty the earth was called by
the same name.   The father of these, Hypsistus,
[*or* ELIOUN], having been killed through an en-

---

[1] Sydyk.   Hebrew צַדִּיק (Tsadik), means *the righteous
one.*   Wagner thinks by this name is designated not any
man, but the institution of law and civil government.

[2] El 'Elyōn is the title given to the god of Melchizedek,
King of Salem, who is called priest of El 'Elyōn, which
our version renders priest of the Most High God.

[3] Perhaps Berith, which in Hebrew signifies *a covenant*
or *engagement*, whence a Phœnician deity was called Baal-
Berith, like the Zeus Orkios of the Greeks, and the Deus
Fidius of the Romans.   This legend of El 'Elyōn and
Berith (covenant), seems to me an obscure allusion to what
is related in Genesis xiv. 18—24.

counter with wild beasts, was consecrated [*i.e.* deified], and his children offered libations and sacrifices to him. But Ouranos succeeding to the kingdom of his father, contracted marriage with his sister Gē (the Earth), and had by her four sons, Ilus who is called Kronus,[1] and Betylus, and Dagon, which signifies Siton (*corn*), and Atlas. But, by other wives, Ouranos had much issue ; at which Gē being vexed and jealous, reproached Ouranos, so that they parted from each other. But Ouranos, though separated from her, still by force came, and had intercourse with her, whenever he pleased, and then went home again. But, when he also attempted to kill the children he had by her, Gē also often defended, or avenged herself, gathering unto her auxiliary powers. But when Kronus came to man's estate, by the advice and assistance of Hermes Trismegistus,[2] who was his secretary, he opposed his father Ouranos, avenging his mother. And Kronus had children, Persephone,[3] and Athena [Minerva]; the former died a virgin ; but, by the advice of Athene and Hermes [*i.e.* Mercury] Kronus made of iron a scimitar, and a spear. Then Hermes [or *Thoth,*] addressing the allies of Kronus with magic words, wrought in them

---

[1] Kronus answers to the Saturn of the Romans.

[2] Or, Thoth, *i.e.*, the thrice great Hermes.

[3] Proserpine.

a keen desire to fight against Ouranos[1] in behalf of
Gē.  And thus Kronus, overcoming Ouranos in battle, drove him from his kingdom, and succeeded him
in the imperial power.  In the battle was taken a
well-beloved concubine of Ouranos, who was pregnant ; Kronus gave her in marriage to Dagon,[2] and
she was delivered, and called the child Demaroon.
After these events Kronus builds a wall round about
his habitation, and founds Byblus,[3] the first city in
Phœnicia.  Afterwards Kronus, suspecting his own
brother Atlas, by the advice of Hermes [or Thoth],
threw him into a deep cavern in the earth, and buried
him.  At this time the descendants of the Dioscuri,
having built some light, and other more complete,
ships, put to sea, and being out over against Mount
Cassius, there consecrated a temple.  But the auxili-

---

[1] *i.e.,* Heaven.

[2] Dagon is represented in 1 Samuel v. 4, as an idol of
the Philistines, with fish's tail ; but in Genesis xxvii. 28,
nearly the same word means *corn*—the one being Dagon,
the other *dagan* [דָּגָן].

[3] Byblus, the modern Jebail, is here represented as the
most ancient city of the Canaanites.  It was celebrated
for the worship of  Tammuz, or Adonis ; who, in the
same manner as Elioun, is said to have been slain in an
encounter with wild beasts.  The mysterious rites of this
worship even infected the Jews.  (See Ezekiel viii. 14.)
Byblus was famous for its celebration of the mysteries of
Adonis, which even passed to Athens.

aries of Ilus, (who is Kronus), were called Elohim,[1] (as it were) the allies of Kronus ; they were so called after Kronus [IL or EL]. And Kronus, having a son called Sadidus, dispatched him with his own sword, because he held him in suspicion ; and with his own hand deprived his son of life. And in like manner he cut off the head of his own daughter, so that all the gods were amazed at the mind of Kronus. But, in process of time, Ouranos, being in banishment, sent his daughter Astarte, with two other sisters, Rhea and Dione, to cut off Kronus by deceit ; but Kronus took the damsels, and married them, being his own sisters. Ouranos understanding this, sent Eimarmene and Hora, with other auxiliaries, to make war against him : but Kronus gained the affections of these also, and kept them with himself. Moreover, the god Ouranos devised Baetulia, contriving stones that moved as having life.[2] And to Kronus was born by Astarte

---

[1] Elohim is the plural of Eloâh = god. This plural, (which some regard as a pluralis excellentiæ), is the word constantly used in the Hebrew Scriptures for *God*. Some, on the other hand, have hence inferred the original polytheism of the Jews.

[2] Baetulia. Instead of λιθους εμψυχους, *i.e.*, *animated* stones, as Philo has rendered it, we may, I think, with Orelli, believe that Sanchoniathon had written אֲבָנִים נְשָׁפִים (AVANIM NESHAPHIM), *anointed stones*, from the root שׁוּף (SHOOPH), used in Syriac (2 Samuel xii. 20, and xiv. 2) in

seven daughters, called Titanides, or Artemides ; and again to him were born by Rhea seven sons, the youngest of whom was consecrated from his birth ; also by Dione he had daughters, and by Astarte again two sons, Pothos, [or Desire], and Eros [or Cupid]. And Dagon after he had found out bread-corn and the plough, was called Jupiter Arotrius (*i.e.*, *the plougher*). To Sydyk, called the Just, one of the Titanides, [or daughters of Titan by Astarte], bare Asclepius (*Æsculapius, god of medicine.*) To Kronus, also, three sons were born in Peræa, (*a district of Syria east of the river Jordan*,) viz., Kronus, of the same name with his father, Jupiter-Belus and Apollo.

---

the sense of *anointing*. Philo, by transposing the letters מ and ש, has completely altered the meaning of the author he undertakes to translate, and rendered him ridiculous. By this transposition the stones which Jacob set up at Bethel for a pillow, and which subsequently, when anointed, he consecrated to God (as we read, Genesis xxviii. 18), have become in Philo's translation *animated* instead of *anointed* stones. Such stones, called Baitylia, of a spherical form, were consecrated, we are told by Nicolaus of Damascus, to various gods. We are, however, to understand in this passage of Sanchoniathon, according to Orelli, either aërolites, or more probably, as he thinks, stones which, by a superstitious notion of the ancients, were supposed to contain some divine or spiritual essence, such as the Pessinuntian stone sent by Attalus, King of Phrygia, to the Romans, in which Cybele, "the mother of the gods," was believed to lie concealed. See Livy's Roman History, Book xxix. 11 and xiv., and Arnobius, advers. Gentes, Book vii. chap. 46.

Contemporary with these were Pontus and Typhon ;
and Nereus, the father of Pontus. From Pontus
descended Sidon, who by the excellence of her singing first invented the hymns of odes or praises ; and
Poseidon [*i.e.* Neptune]. But to Demaroon was born
Melicarthus, who is also called Heracles [Hercules].
Afterwards Ouranos again makes war against Pontus,
but parting from him attaches himself to Demaroon.
Demaroon attacks Pontus ; but Pontus puts him to
flight, and Demaroon vows a sacrifice for his escape.
In the thirty-second year of his power and reign,
Ilus, who is Kronus, having laid an ambuscade for
his father Ouranos in a certain place in the middle
of the earth, and having gotten him into his hands,
cuts off his private parts near fountains and rivers.
There Ouranos was consecrated,[1] and his spirit was
separated, and the blood of his private parts dropped
into the fountains and the waters of the rivers ; and
the place is shewn even to this day. *Then our author,
after mentioning some other matters, proceeds thus :*
' But Astarte, called the greatest, and Demaroon entitled Zeus, (Jupiter), and Adodus named the "king
of the gods," reigned over the country by the consent
of Kronus. And Astarte put upon her head,[2] as a

---

[1] *i.e.,* deified.

[2] Whence in Bashan a city sacred to Astarte was called
(Gen. xiv. 5) ASHTEROTH-KARNAIM ; *i.e., Astarte with the
two horns,* or, the crescent moon.

mark of sovereignty, a bull's head ; and when she
was travelling about the habitable world, she found a
star falling through the air, which she took up and
consecrated in the holy island of Tyre ;[1] and the
Phœnicians say that Astarte is Aphrodite [or Venus].
And Kronus also going about the habitable world,
gave to his daughter Athena [or Minerva], the kingdom of Attica : and when a plague and mortality
happened, Kronus offered up his only son as a sacrifice to his father Ouranos, and circumcised himself,

---

[1] Tyre was regarded as a holy city. In support of this
we have the testimony of Arrian, who says, in his Expedition of Alexander the Great: " There was in that city
(Tyre), a temple dedicated to Hercules (Melkarth), the most
ancient of all those recorded in history. This is not the
Grecian Hercules, for he was the son of Alcmena. But
this Hercules, (Baal or Melkarth), was worshipped at Tyre
many ages before Cadmus sailed from Phœnicia and seized
Thebes (in Bœotia), and long before Semele was born to
Cadmus. Nevertheless, the Hercules worshipped by the
Iberians (Spaniards), at Tartessus, who gave the name to
the pillars of Hercules (the Straits of Gibraltar), is, in my
opinion, the same with the Tyrian. For Tartessus
was built by the Phœnicians, and a temple was reared
there, and sacrifices performed to Hercules after the
Phœnician manner." Again, in Book ii., chap. 24,
"They who had fled to the temple of Hercules (being
some of the chief nobility of Tyre, besides King
Azelmicus, and some Carthaginian priests, who, according to ancient custom, were sent to their mother-city
to offer sacrifices to Hercules) had the benefit of a free
pardon."

and compelled his allies to do the same :[1] and not long afterwards he consecrated after his death another son, named Muth,[2] whom he had by Rhea.[3] The Phœnicians call him Death and Pluto. After these things Kronus, gives the city of Byblus [Hebrew *Gebal*], to the goddess Baaltis,[4] who is also called Dione ;[5] and Berytus[6] he gave to Poseidon [or Nep-

---

[1] What relation Kronus or Saturn may really bear to Abraham it is difficult to say ; but there are certain points of resemblance which are quite unmistakable. 1st, Kronus and Abraham both offer up a son in sacrifice, (Isaac being only saved at the last moment by a special intervention); 2nd, both circumcise themselves ; 3rd, both compel their dependents to do the same.

[2] The god or genius of Death ; *i.e.*, Pluto. מוּת, MÛTH, in this sense, occurs in Psalm xlviii. 15. Eng. Vers. 14. See also Ps. xlix. 14.

[3] A daughter of Ouranos and Gē, or heaven and earth, and wife of Kronus or Saturn.

[4] In Hebrew this would be בַּעֲלַת (BAALATH), *the wife*, viz., of Baal. She was hence, according to Hesychius, either Juno or Venus. She was worshipped in Carthage as Queen of Heaven, as also by the idolatrous Jews.— See Jeremiah vii. 18 and xliv. 17.

[5] Dione is also a daughter of Ouranos and Gē, or heaven and earth. In classical mythology she is represented as beloved by Jupiter, to whom she bore Venus. Homer represents Dione as receiving her wounded daughter with caresses and consolations, and threatening Diomede with a wretched future.

[6] Berytus, once a famous seat of law and learning, now the seaport for Damascus. It is now called Beyroot.

tune], and the Cabiri,[1] the husbandmen and fishermen : and they consecrated the remains[2] of Pontus at
Berytus. But before these things the god Taautus,
having represented Ouranos, made types of the
countenances of the gods Kronus and Dagon, and
the sacred characters of the other elements. He
contrived also for Kronus the ensign of his royal
power, having four eyes in the parts before and in
the parts behind, two of them closing as in sleep ;
and upon the shoulders four wings, two in the act of
flying, and two reposing as at rest. And the symbol
was, that Kronus whilst he slept was watching, and
reposed whilst he was awake. And in like manner
with respect to his wings, that whilst he rested
he was flying, yet rested whilst he flew. But to
the other gods there were two wings only to each
upon his shoulders, to intimate that they flew under
the control of Kronus ; he had also two wings upon
his head, the one for the most governing part, the
mind, and one for the sense. And Kronus coming

---

[1] The Cabiri, or Great Gods, eight in number, were
mysterious deities, who were especially venerated at
Lemnos, and at Samothrace. The worship of the Cabiri
extended to all the western parts of the ancient world.
Hence, we read of Bœotian, Egyptian, Macedonian,
Etruscan, and Pelasgian Cabiri. They were especially
invoked by sailors, and eventually confounded with the
Dioscuri, i.e., Castor and Pollux.

[2] The first instance on record of the consecration of relics.
Bp. Cumberland, in loc.

into the country of the south, gave all Egypt to the god Taautus [or Thoth], that it might be his kingdom. " These things," says Sanchoniathon, "the Cabiri, the seven sons of Sydyk, and their eighth brother Asclepius, [or Esmun, *i.e.*, the eighth], first of all set down in memoirs, as the god Taautus [Thoth] commanded them. All these things the son of Thabion,[1] the first hierophant of all among the Phœnicians, allegorized, and mixed up with the occurrences and passions of nature and the world, and delivered to the priests and prophets, the superintendents of the mysteries : and they, perceiving the rage for these allegories increase, delivered them to their successors, and to foreigners : of whom one was Isiris,[2] the inventor of the three letters, the brother of Chna,[3] who is called the first Phœnician."

To the last fragment, being of a very remarkable character, we append Jacob Bryant's Dissertation :—

" After having shewn that this is the only sacrifice

---

[1] By the son of Thabion both Cumberland and Wagner understand Sanchoniathon himself ; but Orelli, with more probability, thinks that Jerombaal or Jerubaal, priest of the god IAO, is meant. Whether the same as Gideon, who is also called Jerubaal (Judges vi. 32) cannot be decided.

[2] By the name Isiris Cumberland thinks Misor, or Mizraim, the brother of Taut, or Thoth, is meant.

[3] *i.e.*, Canaan, the native name for Phœnicia, as we find on the Phœnician coins of Laodicea ad Libanum.—See my article " Phœnician Language and Inscriptions," in the Supplement (Arts and Sciences) to the *English Cyclo.* 1874.

among the ancients, which is termed *mystical ;* and that Kronus, the personage who offers it was the chief deity of the Phœnicians ; and moreover, that it could not relate to any previous transaction, he concludes thus :—

" The mystical sacrifice of the Phœnicians had these requisites, that a *prince was to offer it ;* and *his only son was to be the victim :* and as I have shewn that this could not relate to any thing *prior ;* let us consider what is said upon the subject, as *future,* and attend to the consequence. For if the sacrifice of the *Phœnicians* was a type of *another* to come, the nature of this last will be known from the representation by which it was prefigured. According to this, *El,* the supreme deity, whose associates were the Elohim, was in process of time to have a son, αγαπητον, well-beloved : μονογενη, his only begotten : who was to be conceived (of ανωβρετ), as some render it, of *grace :* but according to my interpretation, of *the fountain of light.* He was to be called *Jeoud* [or יָחִיד, *i.e., only*] whatever that name may relate to ; and to be *offered up as a sacrifice to his father* λυτρον, by way of *satisfaction,* and *redemption,* τιμωροις δαιμοσι, *to atone for the sins of others,* and *avert the just vengeance of God ;* αντι της παντων φθορας, to prevent universal corruption, and at the same time, *general ruin.* And it is farther remarkable ; *he was to make the grand sacrifice invested with the emblems of royalty.*" Bryant thinks it must be

allowed to be "a type of something to come ;" pre-
figuring, as he supposes, the offering of Christ upon
Calvary.

### FROM PORPHYRY.

Taaut, whom the Egyptians call Thoth, when he
flourished among the Phœnicians with great fame
for his wisdom, arranged in elegant order, and in a
scientific manner, those things which belong to religion, and the worship of the gods, first vindicated
from the ignorance of the lower classes and the
heads of the people. To whom, when the god Sur-
mubelus, and Thuro, who afterwards by a change of
name was called Chrusarthes, succeeded, after a long
interval of ages, they illustrated his secret theology,
which had hitherto been involved in the shades of
allegory. A little after, Sanchoniathon proceeds
thus—

### OF THE MYSTICAL SACRIFICE OF THE PHŒNICIANS.

" It was the custom among the ancients, in times of
great calamity, in order to prevent the ruin of all, for
the rulers of the city or nation to sacrifice to the
avenging deities the most beloved of their children,
as the price of redemption : they who were devoted
for this purpose were offered mystically. For Kronus
or (Saturn), whom the Phœnicians call Israel,[1] and
who after his death was deified, and instated in the

---

[1] *Quære*, Il ?

planet which bears his name, when he was king, had by a nymph of the country, called Anobret,[1] an only son, who, on that account is styled Ieoud ;[2] for, so the Phœnicians still call an only son : and when great danger from war beset the land, he adorned the altar, and invested this son with the emblems of royalty, and sacrificed him.—*From Eusebius' Præp. Evang.* lib. i. cap. x.

### FROM PHILO-BYBLIUS, OR PORPHYRY,

(*It is uncertain*),

*But, according to Wagner and others, this Fragment is, most probably, from Porphyry.*

## ON THE SERPENT.

Taautus first consecrated the basilisk, and introduced the worship of the serpent-tribe ; in which he was followed by the Phœnicians and Egyptians. For this animal was held by him to be the most inspirited of all the reptiles, and of a fiery nature ; inasmuch as it exhibits an incredible celerity, moving by its spirit without either hands, or feet, or any of those external organs, by which other animals effect their motion.   And in its progress it assumes

---

[1] *i.e., Conceiving by favour,* as interpreted by Bochart. By this name he thinks Sarah, the wife of Abraham, is intended.

[2] יָחִיד, YAKHÌD, *only-begotten,* or *only son.* See the Hebrew text of Gen. xxii. 2.

a variety of forms, moving in a spiral course, and at what degree of swiftness it pleases. And it is very long-lived, and has the quality not only of putting off its old age, and assuming a second youth ; but it receives a greater increase. And when it has fulfilled the appointed measure of its existence, it consumes itself, as Taautus has laid down in the sacred books, wherefore this animal is introduced in the sacred rites and mysteries.—*Euseb. Præp. Evang.*, Bk. i., chap. 10.

*End of the Fragments of Sanchoniathon.*

# THE FRAGMENTS

OF

# THE TYRIAN ANNALS:

FROM

## DIUS AND MENANDER.

# THE TYRIAN ANNALS.

## FROM DIUS.

"UPON the death of Abibalus his son Hiromus [Hiram] succeeded to the kingdom. He raised the eastern parts of the city, and enlarged it; and joined to it the temple of Jupiter Olympius,[1] which stood before upon an island, by filling up the intermediate space: and he adorned that temple with donations of gold: and he went up into Libanus [Lebanon], to cut timber for the construction of the temples. And it is said that Solomon, king of Jerusalem, sent enigmas to Hiromus [Hiram], and desired others in return, with a proposal that whichsoever of the two

---

[1] Or Melkarth, *i.e.*, *King of the City*, the Baal of Tyre. To this deity a very ancient and richly adorned temple was erected, which was renowned throughout the world. Annual gifts were sent thither from Carthage and the most distant Phœnician colonies. During my residence at Safed, in Galilee, in 1855, a great treasure of Tyrian coins was discovered, some of the finest of which I purchased. On one side was seen, beautifully executed, the head of the Tyrian Baal; on the other an eagle (the symbol of the Syro-Macedonian dynasty, which at that time governed Tyre), with the inscription in Greek, which being translated reads, "Of Tyre a holy city and asylum."

was unable to solve them, should forfeit money to
the other. Hiromus [Hiram], agreed to the proposal, but was unable to solve the enigmas, and paid
a large sum as a forfeit. And it is said that one
Abdemonus, a Tyrian, solved the enigmas, and pro-
posed others which Solomon was not able to unriddle,
for which he repaid the fine to Hiromus [Hiram]."—
*Joseph. contr. Ap.* lib. i. c. 17.—*Syncel. Chron.* 182.

*End of the Fragment from Dius.*

---

### FROM MENANDER.

" AFTER the death of Abibalus, Hiromus [Hiram]
his son succeeded him in his kingdom, and reigned
thirty-four years, having lived fifty-three. He laid
out that part of the city which is called Eurychoron :[1]
and consecrated the golden column which is in the
temple of Jupiter.[2] And he went up into the forest

---

[1] Literally, the *broad dance*. It designates, no doubt, an
open space, as a square or promenade.

[2] Jupiter Belus, or Olympius ; *i.e.*, the Tyrian Baal. By
some writers he is called the Tyrian Hercules. From this
deity the two mountains on the Strait of Gibraltar are
called the Pillars of Hercules—Abyla on the one side and
Calpe on the other—for, so far the Tyrian Hercules (or
Baal) is said to have carried his conquests; in other words, so
far did Phœnician commerce, at a very early period, extend.

on the mountain called Libanus [Lebanon], to fell
cedars for the roofs of the temples : and having demolished the ancient temples, he rebuilt them, and
consecrated the fanes [or temples] of Hercules [*i.e.*,
Baal] and Astarte : he constructed that of Hercules
first, in the month Peritius [*i.e.*, February] ; then that
of Astarte, when he had overcome the Tityans who
had refused to pay their tribute : and when he had
reduced them he returned. In his time was a certain young man named Abdemonus, who used to
solve the problems which were propounded to him
by Solomon, king of Jerusalem."—*From Josephus
contra Apion*, lib. i. cap. 18 ; *and Josephus Antiq.
Jud.* lib. viii. cap. 5.

## OF THE SUCCESSORS OF HIRAM.

" Upon the death of Hiromus [Hiram], Baleazarus
his son, succeeded to the kingdom ; he lived forty-
three years, and reigned seven. After him, Abdas-
tratus [Abd-Astarte], his son, reigned nine years,
having lived twenty-nine. Against him the four sons
of his nurse conspired and slew him. Of these, the
eldest reigned twelve years. After them Astartus,
the son of Delæastartus, reigned twelve years, having
lived fifty-four. After him his brother Aserumus,
reigned nine years, having lived fifty-four. He was
slain by his brother Pheles, who governed the king-

dom eight months, having lived fifty years. He was
murdered by a priest of Astarte, Ithobalus [Ethbaal],
who reigned thirty-two years, having lived sixty-
eight. He was succeeded by his son, Badezorus,
who reigned six years, having lived forty-five. His
successor was Matgenus, his son, who reigned nine
years, having lived thirty-two. He was succeeded by
Phygmalion, who reigned forty-seven years, having
lived fifty-six. In the seventh year of his reign, his
sister (*Dido*), fled from him, and founded the city of·
Carthage in Libya (B.C. 878).—*From Josephus contra
Apion*, lib. i. cap. 18.

---

OF THE INVASION OF SALMANASAR (OR SHALMANESER.)

" ELULÆUS[1] reigned thirty-six years : and he fitted
out a fleet against the Kittæans (Chittim or Cypriots)
who had revolted, and reduced them to obedience.
But Salmanasar, the king of the Assyrians, sent them
assistance, and overran Phœnicia : and when he had
made peace with the Phœnicians he returned with all

---

[1] Called LULIA, in the cuneiform inscription of Sennacherib (Taylor cylinder line 35). This interesting historical
document has been translated into English, and will be
found at p. 35 of vol. i. of " Records of the Past." Norris,

his forces. And Sidon, and Aké,[1] and Palætyrus,[2] and many other cities revolted from the Tyrians, and put themselves under the protection of the king of Assyria. But as the Tyrians still refused to submit, the king made another expedition against them : and the Phœnicians furnished him with sixty ships and eighty gallies : and the Tyrians attacked him with twelve ships, and dispersed the hostile fleet, and took prisoners to the amount of five hundred men : upon which account the Tyrians were held in great respect. But the king of Assyria stationed guards upon the river and at the aqueducts, to prevent the Tyrians from drawing water : and this continued five years, during all which time they were obliged to drink from wells which they dug."—*Joseph. Antiq. Jud.* lib. ix. c. 14.

---

in his *Assyrian Dictionary* (*sub voce* LULI, p. 670), says the name Luliah occurs also in the Bellino cylinder, i. 18, and at line 13 of the Nebbi-Yunas inscription which records the campaigns of Esarhaddon. I do not find the name in either. In the Bellino no mention of Sidon at all, while in the Nebbi-Yunas the King is called Abdi-Milkutti. Josephus (Antiq. ix. 14) calls him Elulaeus, King of *Tyre*.

[1] Acco, now St. Jean d'Acre : the Ptolemais of the New Testament. It occurs in Judges i. 31 ; Micah i. 10 *(Heb. text)*, and 1 Maccab. v. 22.

[2] *i.e.*, Old Tyre.

## OF THE KINGS AND JUDGES FROM NEBUCHADNEZZAR TO CYRUS.

IN the reign of Ithobalus [*or*, Ethbaal[1]], Nabuchodonosorus [Nebuchadnezzar] beseiged Tyre for thirteen years.[2]    After him reigned Baal ten years.
After him Judges [*or* Suffetes], were appointed who
judged the people : Ecnibalus, the son of Balsachus,
two months : Chelbes, the son of Abdæus, ten
months : Abbarus, the high-priest, three months :
Mytgonus and Gerastratus the son of Abdelemus,
six years : after them Balatorus reigned one year.
After his death they sent to fetch Merbalus from
Babylon ; and he reigned four years : and when he
died they sent for Hiromus [Hiram], his brother,
who reigned twenty years.    In his time Cyrus was
king of Persia."—*Joseph. contr. Ap.* lib. i. cap. 21.

---

[1] Ethbaal seems to have been a common Phœnician
name.   The first Tyrian king of this name gave his
daughter Jezebel, (whence our name Isabella), to wife to
Ahab, King of Israel.   The sovereign here mentioned
transferred the seat of government to Tyre on the island,
which, in the time of Alexander the Great, was joined to
Old Tyre on the mainland.

[2] Menander does not say that at the end of the time the
city was taken. We learn this, however, from other sources,
although some, from the silence of Menander, have inferred
that Nebuchadnezzar raised the siege and departed without
capturing Tyre.

*End of the Fragments from Menander.*

# THE PERIPLUS

OF

# HANNO.

THE PERIPLUS OF HANNO THE CARTHAGINIAN is an account of the earliest voyage of discovery in existence. It is taken from an original, and apparently, official document, which was suspended in the temple of Il, or Saturn, at Carthage. Falconer and Bougainville both agree in referring it to the sixth century before the Christian era. The Periplus is introduced by a few lines, reciting a decree of the Carthaginians, relating to the voyage and its objects. It is then continued as a narrative by the commander, or by one of his companions, commencing from the time the fleet had cleared the Pillars of Hercules —the Straits of Gibraltar.

# THE PERIPLUS[1] OF HANNO.

## THE VOYAGE OF HANNO, COMMANDER OF THE CARTHAGINIANS.

ROUND the parts of Libya beyond the Pillars of Hercules,[2] which he deposited in the temple of Saturn [*i.e.*, Il, *or* Israel.]

It was decreed by the Carthaginians, that Hanno should undertake a voyage beyond the pillars of Hercules, and found Libyphœnician cities. He sailed accordingly with sixty ships of fifty oars each, and a body of men and women to the number of thirty thousand, and provisions and other necessaries.

When we had passed the Pillars [of Hercules] on our voyage, and had sailed beyond them for two days, we founded the first city, which we named Thymiaterium.[3] Below it lay an extensive plain. Proceeding thence towards the west, we came to

---

[1] Derived from περι around, and πλους a sailing, a voyage; hence Periplus = a circumnavigation.

[2] The mountains Abyla and Calpe, situated on either side of the Strait of Gibraltar, were called by the ancients the Pillars of Hercules.

[3] Probably Mogadore.

Soloeis,[1] a promontory of Libya, a place thickly
covered with trees, where we erected a temple to
Neptune ; and again proceeded for the space of half
a day towards the east, until we arrived at a lake
lying not far from the sea, and filled with abundance
of large reeds.  Here elephants, and a great number
of other wild beasts were feeding.  Having passed
the lake about a day's sail, we founded cities near
the sea, called Cariconticos, and Gytte, and Acra,
and Melitta, and Arambys.  Thence we came to
the great river Lixus,[2] which flows from Libya.  On
its banks the Lixitæ, a shepherd-tribe, were feeding
flocks, amongst whom we continued some time on
friendly terms.  Beyond the Lixitæ dwelt the inhos-
pitable Ethiopians, who pasture a wild country intersected by large mountains, from which, they say, the
river Lixus flows.  In the neighbourhood of the
mountains lived the Troglodytæ,[3] men of various
appearances, whom the Lixitæ described as swifter
in running than horses.  Having procured interpreters from them, we coasted along a desert country,
towards the south, for two days.  Thence we proceeded towards the east the course of a day.  Here
we found in a recess of a certain bay a small island,

---

[1] Cape Bojador.

[2] Supposed to be identical with the River d'Ouro ; or
Rio d'Ouro.

[3] *i.e.*, Dwellers in caves.

containing a circle of five stadia, where we settled a
colony, and called it Kerne.[1]   We judged from our
voyage that this place lay in a direct line with Carthage ; for the length of our voyage from Carthage to
the Pillars, was equal to that from the Pillars to Kerne.

We then came to a lake which we reached by
sailing up a large river called Chretes.[2]   This lake
had three islands, larger than Kerne ; from which
proceeding a day's sail, we came to the extremity of
the lake, that was overhung by large mountains,
inhabited by savage men, clothed in skins of wild
beasts, who drove us away by throwing stones, and
hindered us from landing.   Sailing thence we came
to another river,[3] that was large and broad, and full
of crocodiles, and river-horses ; whence returning
back we came again to Kerne.

Thence we sailed towards the south twelve days,
coasting the shore, the whole of which is inhabited
by Ethiopians, who would not wait our approach, but
fled from us.   Their language was not intelligible,
even to. the Lixitæ who were with us.   Towards
the last day we approached some large mountains
covered with trees, the wood of which was sweet-
scented and variegated.   Having sailed by these

---

[1] Probably, the island of Arguin, under the southern
Cape Blanco.

[2] Perhaps the river St. John.

[3] Perhaps the river Senegal.

mountains for two days, we came to an immense
opening of the sea ; on each side of which, towards
the continent, was a plain ; from which we saw, by
night, fire arising, at intervals, in all directions,
either more or less. Having taken in water there,
we sailed forwards for five days near the land, until
we came to a large bay, which our interpreters
informed us was called the Western Horn.[1] In this
was a large island, and in the island a salt-water
lake, and in this another island, where, when we had
landed, we could discover nothing in the day-time
except trees ; but in the night we saw many fires
burning, and heard the sound of pipes, cymbals,
drums, and confused shouts. We were then afraid,
and our diviners ordered us to abandon the island.
Sailing quickly away thence, we passed a country
burning with fires and perfumes ; and streams of fire
supplied from it fell into the sea. The country was
impassable on account of the heat. We sailed
quickly thence, being much terrified ; and passing
on for four days, we discovered at night a country
full of fire. In the middle was a lofty fire, larger
than the rest, which seemed to touch the stars.
When day came, we discovered it to be a large hill,
called the Chariot of the Gods.[2] On the third day
after our departure thence, having sailed by those

---

[1] Probably Cape Palmas.    [2] Perhaps Sierra Leone.

streams of fire, we arrived at a bay called the Southern Horn;[1] at the bottom of which lay an island like the former, having a lake, and in this lake another island, full of savage people, (the greater part of whom were women), whose bodies were hairy, and whom our interpreters called Gorillæ. Though we pursued the men we could not seize any of them ; but all fled from us, escaping over the precipices, and defending themselves with stones. Three women were, however, taken ; but they attacked their conductors with their teeth and hands, and could not be prevailed upon to accompany us. Having killed them, we flayed them, and brought their skins with us to Carthage.   We did not sail further on, our provisions failing us.

*End of the Periplus of Hanno.*

---

[1] Probably Cape Three Points.

# THE FRAGMENTS

OF

# THE CHALDÆAN HISTORY:

FROM

## BEROSSUS, ABYDENUS, AND MEGASTHENES.

Berosus, or Berossus, for his name is variously written by ancient writers, was a priest of Bel, and most probably a native of Babylon. His name may be from בְּרוֹשׁ (BEROSH) a fir-tree; בַּר אָסְיָא (BAR ASYA) *i.e.*, "Son of the Physician;" or, as the learned Scaliger conjectured, from BAR, or BIR, *Son*, and *Hosea*, hence "Son of Hosea."

If the latter be the correct etymology, he may have been of Jewish origin. By some he is made to be a contemporary of Alexander the Great; but it is more probable that he flourished in the reign of Ptolemy Philadelphus, King of Egypt. Justin Martyr will have it that he was the father of the Cumæan Sibyl, who lived in the reign of Tarquinius Superbus; but the most probable opinion, and the best supported, is that of Tatian, the Assyrian, who tells us that Berosus dedicated his *Three Books of Chaldean History* to Antiochus Soter, King of Syria. (Tatian: *Oratio contra Græcos*) (Αντιοχῳ τῷ μετ' αυτον τρίτῳ) which Eusebius has altered into Αντιόχῳ τῷ μετα Σελευκον τριτῳ. George, the Syncellus, of Byzantium, states that Berosus lived at the same time as Manetho the Egyptian, or a little before; and Manetho, we know, was a contemporary of Ptolemy Philadelphus, who began his reign over Egypt, B.C. 284, and reigned 38 years; whence the learned Scaliger has endeavoured to prove that Berosus may have lived from the time of Alexander the Great to the 13th year of Antiochus Soter, King of Syria, and even beyond that period. Our author was held in great repute by ancient writers, and his authority was great with both Greek and Latin authors. Tatian confesses that he had not himself read the works of Berosus, but frankly acknowledges that he is indebted for the information he gives of him to Juba ii., King of Mauritania, who had written a history of the Assyrians. Vitruvius (Book ix., chap. 1) informs us that having left Babylon upon the conquest of that city by Alexander, and being acquainted with the Greek language, Berosus established himself in Asia Minor, intending to teach Oriental science. Thence he removed to the island of Cos, where he had an observatory, and opened a school of astronomy, which at that period also comprehended astrology.

To him, says Pliny (Natural History, vii. 37), the Athenians erected a statue in the Gymnasium with a gilded tongue, on account of his astronomical knowledge, and the wonderful accuracy of his predictions. He is also credited by Vitruvius with the invention of some kind of astronomical clock. [Hemicyclium excavatum ex quadrato ad enclimaque succisum Berosus Chaldæus dicitur invenisse.] Pliny tells us that the genuine works of our author

contained astronomical observations for a space of
480 years, *i.e.*, from Nabonassar to B.C. 270. All
his works have perished except a few fragments;
but it is unanimously agreed among ancient writers
that the Berosus who wrote the history of the
Chaldeans, also wrote various astronomical treatises.
Josephus, Plutarch, Eusebius, George the Syncellus,
Athenæus, Pliny, Seneca, Pausanias, Jerome, and
many other ancient authors, have expressly mentioned our author, or have given quotations from
his works. We cannot, however, deny that many of
the fragments of Berosus which have come down to
us, have been more or less corrupted, sometimes
through the carelessness of copyists, at others inten-
tionally to serve the writer's purpose. Whether he
had ever seen the Hebrew Scriptures is very uncertain. Josephus says that he made mention of
Abraham, but without expressly naming him, calling
him "a just and great man among the Chaldeans,
who lived in the 10th generation after the flood,"
and saying that he was an observer of the heavens.

It is certainly very remarkable that he should
have given a description of the Flood in terms so
much resembling the account in the Book of
Genesis, but still more striking that the ten kings
enumerated by Berosus, as reigning before the
Flood, should agree so closely (not in name but in
number), with the ten generations from Adam to
Noah. Noah is represented by Xisuthrus—the

hero of the Deluge, according to Berosus—but who may be meant by Oannes and the Annedoti, it is very difficult to say. Berosus, as priest of the god Bel, would have access to the temple archives, and therefore whatever is stated by him is of the highest importance.

We have the names of a dynasty of Chaldean kings handed down to us, supposed by some to be from Berosus. These are

EVECHOUS, who reigned 6 years.
CHOMASBOLUS    „    7    „
PORUS    „    35    „
NECHOBES    „    43    „
ABIUS    „    45    „
ONIBALLUS    „    40    „
ZINZIRUS    „    45    „

George the Syncellus also gives a list of the Arab dynasty, consisting of six kings, who reigned over Babylon; but whence he obtained it we are not informed. These are

MARDOKENTES, who reigned 45 years.
SISIMADACUS    „    28    „
GABIUS    „    37    „
PARANNOS    „    40    „
NABONNABOS    „    25    „
——— (name lost)    „    41    „

Among the thousands of cuneiform inscriptions deposited in the British Museum, there are very few which contain any general chronology of the Assyrio-Babylonian Empire, although we possess a few which give the number of years that had elapsed between particular and important events. Our Museum rejoices, however, in the possession of some precious fragments of a *Synchronous History of Babylon and Assyria*, which describes the wars, treaties, and other important transactions between the kingdoms of Babylonia and Assyria during several centuries, but we have no connected and continuous history.

This most important document was translated and in part published by Sir Henry Rawlinson some years ago. A translation of the whole of it, including some recently-discovered fragments, translated by Rev. A. H. Sayce, is now to be found in the *Transactions of the Society of Biblical Archæology*, vol. ii. pt. i., and again republished in *Records of the Past*, vol. iii., p. 25.

Then we have another most valuable aid to Assyrian chronology in the Assyrian Canon,[1] which extends, however, only from B.C. 909 to B.C. 680, comprising a period of about 230 years, the chronology of which is confirmed and verified by a solar eclipse therein mentioned, and which we know happened on June 15th, B.C. 763. Translations of this Canon were published in the *Athenæum* (Nos. 1812 and 2064) by Sir Henry Rawlinson, and subsequently in a more complete form by Schrader in his admir-

---

[1] *The Assyrian Canon*, by George Smith. Bagster, 1875.

able work entitled, *Die Keilinschriften und Das Alte Testament.*—Leipzig, 1869.

It had long been a matter of speculation among scholars as to the source whence Berosus drew his information regarding the early times of the Babylonian Empire. The general opinion, however, was that in his capacity of priest of Bel, he had access in the temple to documents unknown to the vulgar, whilst the spread of the Greek language in Asia through the Macedonian conquests, furnished him with an enquiring public who would welcome such information, drawn as it were out of the mysterious darkness of Babylonian temples. Such opinion has quite recently met with a remarkable confirmation. Mr. George Smith, of the British Museum, the able decipherer of the Deluge, and other cuneiform tablets, has announced, in the *Transactions of the Society of Biblical Archæology,* that he has discovered what he believes to be the very tablets whence the priest of Bel derived his information. If such be not the case, it will at least be very difficult to account for the remarkable agreement which we find upon many points between the statements of Berosus, and the information supplied by the cuneiform tablets.

Thus, the first dynasty of Berosus consists of ten kings who reigned before the flood, answering to the ten antediluvian Patriarchs of the Old Testament. The first name in the list of Berosus is Alorus,

answering to Adi-ur of the cuneiform, which signifies
"devoted to the god Ur." His fifth name is
Amegalarus, which possibly represents the cuneiform Amil-ur-gal, *i.e.*, man, or servant of Urgal. The
last two names of this dynasty are Otiartes and
Xisuthrus answering to the cuneiform Ubara-Tutu
and Si-sit. The former name is given, in one copy
of Berosus, as Ardates, which corresponds to the
Assyrian *ardu* = a servant, while Tutu is the name
of a god; hence, *servant of Tutu*, which is also
the meaning of the Accadian *Ubara-Tutu*. Tsisit
or Sisit is the Hero of the Flood, the history
of which, as given by Berosus, so remarkably corresponds with the Biblical account of the Noachian
Deluge that no one can doubt that both proceed
from one source—they are evidently transcriptions,
except the names, from some ancient document.
We shall see this brought out more distinctly when
we come to his History of the Deluge. The reading of the name is, however, conjectural,[1] as to the
*pronunciation*, while the *meaning* of the two characters composing it appears to denote *him who
escaped the flood.* .

---

[1] Mr. George Smith has since announced (*Assyrian
Discoveries*, pp. 167, 179, 182) that he has found a tablet
with the name of the hero of the Deluge written phoneti-
cally, KHA-SIS-ADRA; so that Xisuthrus is evidently only
a Greek corruption.

For further information concerning the Fragments
of Berosus we must refer the reader to, "*Berosi
Chaldæorum Historiæ quæ supersunt, cum Com-
mentatione,*" edited by Dr. Richter, Leipzig, 1825,
to which we acknowledge ourselves much indebted,
in regard to the notes and explanations given in this ·
work. We must, however, mention in the highest
terms of commendation, two works which have recently appeared, the one by Mr. George Smith, entitled *The Chaldean Account of Genesis* (London,
1875), being illustrations of the Book of Genesis
from cuneiform sources ; the other an important work
by M. François Lenormant, *Essai de Commentaire
des Fragments Cosmogoniques de Berose, d'après les
Textes Cuneiforms et les Monuments de l'Art
Asiatique.* 8vo. Paris, 1872.

# BEROSUS:

EXTRACTED FROM APOLLODORUS.

## OF THE CHALDÆAN KINGS.

" THIS is the history which Berosus has transmitted to us. He tells us that the first king was Alorus[1] of Babylon, a Chaldæan ; he reigned ten sari[2]; and afterwards Alaparus and Amelon, who came from Pantibiblon[3]; then Ammenon the Chaldæan, in whose time appeared the Musarus Oannes, the Annedotus, from the Erythræan[4] sea. (But Alexander Polyhistor, anticipating the event, has said that he appeared in the first year ; but Apollodorus says that it was after forty sari ; Abydenus, however, makes the second Annedotus appear after twenty-six sari.) Then succeeded Megalarus, from the city of Pantibiblon, and he reigned eighteen sari ; and after him Daonus, the shepherd, from Pantibiblon, reigned ten sari ; in his time, (he says),

---

[1] Ur is the name of an ancient Babylonian deity.

[2] For the explanation of the Babylonian words *saros*, *neros*, and *sossus*, see p. 53 of the present work, line 8th from the top.

[3] This is the Greek rendering of Sippara, called Sepharvaim, or the two Sipparas in our Bible.—2 Kings xvii. 24.

[4] This signifies both the Red Sea and the Persian Gulf. Here it must mean the latter.

appeared again, from the Erythræan (or Red) sea, a fourth Annedotus, having the same form with those above, the shape of a fish blended with that of a man. Then Euedoreschus reigned from the city of Pantibiblon[1] for the period of eighteen sari. In his days there appeared another personage, whose name was Odacon, from the Erythrean (or Red) sea,[2] like the former, having the same complicated form, between a fish and a man. (All these, says Apollodorus, related particularly and circumstantially whatever Oannes had informed them of. Concerning these appearances Abydenus has made no mention.) Then Amempsinus, a Chaldæan from Laranchae,[3] reigned, and he, being the eighth in order, ruled for ten sari. Then Otiartes, a Chaldæan from Laranchae, reigned, and he ruled for eight sari.

Upon the death of Otiartes, his son, Xisuthrus,[4] reigned eighteen sari. In his time the great Flood happened. So the sum total of all the kings is ten ; and the period which they collectively reigned amounts to one hundred and twenty sari.—*Extracted from the Chronicon of Syncellus 39, and Eusebius' Chronicon 5.*

---

[1] Sippara, or Sepharvaim.

[2] The Persian Gulf.

[3] Larissa, the modern Senkereh. The name *Larsā* occurs in a cuneiform inscription of Nebuchadnezzar, now in the British Museum.—See also Xenophon's *Anab.* Bk .iii. c. 4.

[4] *i.e.,* Khasis-Adra.

# BEROSUS:

---

## OF THE CHALDÆAN KINGS AND THE DELUGE.

"So much concerning the wisdom of the Chaldæans.

It is said that the first king of the country was Alorus[1], who gave out a report that he was appointed by God to be the Shepherd of the people: he reigned ten sari. Now a sarus is esteemed to be three thousand six hundred years; a neros, six hundred: and a sossus, sixty.

After him Alaparus reigned three sari; to him succeeded Amillarus, from the city of Pantibiblon, who reigned thirteen sari; in his time a semi-dæmon called Annedotus, very like to Oannes,[2] came up a second time from the sea. After him Ammenon reigned twelve sari, who was of the city of Pantibiblon[3]; then Megalarus, of the same place, eighteen sari; then Daos, the shepherd, governed for the space of ten sari, he was of Pantibiblon; in his time four double-shaped personages came out of the sea to land, whose names were Euedocus, Eneugamus,

---

[1] UR, an ancient Babylonian deity, mentioned in the Cuneiform inscription of Urukh as the eldest son of Bel. —See *Records of the Past*, vol. iii. pp. 9, 10.

[2] Perhaps the god ANU, of the Assyrian inscriptions.

[3] Sippara, or Sepharvaim.

Eneuboulos, and Anementus. After these things was Anodaphus, in the time of Euedoreschus. There were afterwards other kings, and last of all Sisithrus (Xisuthrus). So that, in all, the number amounted to ten kings, and the term of their reigns to one hundred and twenty sari. And, among other matters not irrelevant to the subject, he continues thus concerning the deluge. After Euedoreschus some others reigned, and then Sisithrus (Xisuthrus). To him the god Kronus (*i.e.* Saturn) foretold that, on the fifteenth day of the month Desius there would be a Deluge, and commanded him to deposit all the writings whatever he had in the city of the Sun, in Sippara. Sisithrus (Xisuthrus), when he had complied with these commands, instantly sailed to Armenia, and was immediately inspired by God. During the prevalence of the waters Sisithrus (Xisuthrus) sent out birds that he might judge if the flood had subsided. But the birds passing over an unbounded sea, and not finding any place of rest returned again to Sisithrus. This he repeated ; and when upon the third trial he succeeded, for the birds then returned with their feet stained with mud, the gods translated him from among men. With respect to the vessel, which yet remains in Armenia, it is a custom of the inhabitants to form bracelets and amulets of its wood.—*From Syncellus* 38, *Eusebius, Præpar. Evangel. lib.* IX., *and Eusebius Chronicon* V., 8.

## OF THE TOWER OF BABEL.

" They say that the first inhabitants of the earth, glorying in their own strength and size, and despising the gods, undertook to build a tower, whose top should reach the sky, upon that spot where Babylon now stands. But, when it approached the heaven, the winds assisted the gods, and overturned the work upon its contrivers, (its ruins are said to be at Babylon,) and the gods introduced a diversity of tongues among men, who till that time had all spoken the same language. And a war arose between Kronus (*i.e.* Saturn) and Titan ; and the place in which they built the tower is now called Babylon,[1] on account of the confusion of the languages ; for confusion is by the Hebrews called Babel."—*From Eusebius, Præp. Evangel. lib.* IX. *Syncellus Chron.* 44, *and Eusebius' Chronicon* 13.

---

[1] Babylon is the Greek form of the Assyrian name *Bab-ilu, i.e.,* Gate of God. It was regarded as a holy city. The Hebrew word BILBOOL, resembling *Babilu* in sound, and signifying *confusion,* gave rise to the narrative of the confusion of tongues, and led to the Jewish explanation of the name Babel as connected with that event. A story somewhat similar is found in a cuneiform inscription translated by Mr. Boscawen, and published in the *Trans. Soc. Bib. Arch.,* vol. iv.

# BEROSUS:

FROM ALEXANDER POLYHISTOR.

---

## OF THE COSMOGONY AND CAUSES OF THE DELUGE.

BEROSUS, in his first book concerning the history of Babylonia, informs us that he lived in the time of Alexander, the son of Philip. And he mentions that there were written accounts preserved at Babylon with the greatest care, comprehending a term of fifteen myriads of years. These writings contained a history of the heavens and the sea; of the birth of mankind; also of those who had sovereign rule; and of the actions achieved by them.

And, in the first place, he describes Babylonia as a country which lay between the Tigris and Euphrates. He mentions that it abounded with wheat, barley, ocrus, sesamum; and in the lakes were found the roots called gongæ, which were good to be eaten, and were, in respect to nutriment, like barley. There were also palm-trees and apples, and most kinds of fruits; fish, too, and birds; both those which are merely of flight, and those which take to the element of water. The part of Babylonia which bordered upon Arabia was barren, and without water; but that which lay on the other side had hills, and was fruitful. At Babylon there was (in these times) a great resort of people of various nations, who inhabited Chaldea, and lived without rule and order, like the beasts of the field.

In the first year there made its appearance, from a part of the Erythræan sea[1] which bordered upon Babylonia, an animal endowed with reason, who was called Oannes. (According to the account of Apollodorus) the whole body of the animal was like that of a fish ; and had under a fish's head another head, and also feet below, similar to those of a man, subjoined to the fish's tail. His voice, too, and language was articulate and human ; and a representation of him is preserved even to this day.

This Being, in the day-time, used to converse with men ; but took no food at that season ; and he gave them an insight into letters, and sciences, and every kind of art. He taught them to construct houses, to found temples, to compile laws, and explained to them the principles of geometrical knowledge. He made them distinguish the seeds of the earth, and showed them how to collect fruits. In short, he instructed them in everything which could tend to soften manners and humanise mankind. From that time, so universal were his instructions, nothing material has been added by way of improvement. When the sun set it was the custom of this Being to plunge again into the sea, and abide all night in the deep ; for he was amphibious.

---

[1] The Persian Gulf.

After this, there appeared other animals, like
Oannes, of which Berosus promises to give an
account when he comes to the history of the kings.
Moreover, Oannes wrote concerning the generation
of mankind ; of their different ways of life, and of
their civil polity ; and the following is the purport of
what he said,—

" There was a time in which there was nothing
but darkness and an abyss of waters,[1] wherein resided
most hideous beings, which were produced of a two-
fold principle.   Men appeared with two wings, some
with four wings, and two faces. They had one body,
but two heads—the one of a man, the other of a
woman. They were likewise, in their several organs,
both male and female.   Other human figures were
to be seen with the legs and horns of goats.   Some
had horses' feet ; others had the limbs of a horse
behind, but before were fashioned like men, resembling hippocentaurs. Bulls, likewise, bred there with
the heads of men ; and dogs, with fourfold bodies,
and the tails of fishes.   Also horses, with the heads
of dogs : men, too, and other animals, with the heads
and bodies of horses and the tails of fishes.   In
short, there were creatures with the limbs of every
species of animals.   Add to these fishes, reptiles,
serpents, with other wonderful animals, which
assumed each other's shape and countenance.   Of

---

[1] Compare with Genesis i. 2.

all these were preserved delineations in the temple of Belus at Babylon.

" The person, who was supposed to have presided over them, was a woman named Omoroca[1] ; which in the Chaldee language is Thalatth ; which in Greek is interpreted Thalassa[2], the sea : but, according to the most true computation, it is equivalent to Selene, the moon. All things being in this situation, Belus came, and cut the woman asunder : and, out of one half of her, he formed the earth, and of the other half the heavens ; and at the same time he destroyed the animals in the abyss. All this (he says) was an allegorical description of nature. For the whole universe consisting of moisture, and animals being continually generated therein ; the deity (Belus), above-mentioned, cut off his own head ; upon which the other gods mixed the blood, as it gushed out, with the earth ; and from thence men were formed. On this account it is that men are rational, and partake of divine knowledge. This Belus, whom men call Dis, (or Pluto,) divided the darkness, and separated the heavens from the earth, and reduced the universe to order. But the animals so recently

---

[1] This is a Greek corruption of the Aramaic word, עֲמִיקָא 'Amqia, *i.e.*, the deep ; the ocean.

[2] Thalath, or Thalassa, is evidently τα ἅλς, *i.c.*, τα for tha = the Egyptian feminine article *the*, and the Greek ἅλς, salt—hence, *the sea*.

created, not being able to bear the prevalence of light, died.

Belus upon this, seeing a vast space quite un-inhabited, though by nature very fruitful, ordered one of the gods to take off his head ; and when it was taken off, they were to mix the blood with the soil of the earth, and from thence to form other men and animals, which should be capable of bear-ing the light.  Belus also formed the stars, and the sun and the moon, together with the five planets. (In the second book was the history of the ten kings of the Chaldeans, and the periods of each reign, which consisted collectively of one hundred and twenty sari, or 432,000 years, reaching to the time of the Flood.  For Alexander, surnamed Polyhistor, as from the writings of the Chaldeans, enumerating the kings from the ninth, Ardates, to Xisuthrus, who is called by them the tenth, proceeds in this manner :)

After the death of Ardates, his son, Xisuthrus, succeeded, and reigned eighteen sari.  In his time happened the great Deluge ; the history of which is given in this manner. The Deity, Kronus, appeared to him in a vision, and gave him notice, that upon the fifteenth day of the month Dæsia[1] there would be a flood, by which mankind would be destroyed. He therefore enjoined him to commit to writing a

---

[1] The 5th month of the Macedonian year, answering to May and June.

history of the beginning, progress, and final conclusion of all things, down to the present term ; and
to bury these accounts securely in the city of the
Sun[1] at Sippara ; and to build a vessel, and to take
with him into it his friends and relations ; and to
convey on board everything necessary to sustain
life, and to take in also all species of animals that
either fly, or rove upon the earth ; and trust himself
to the deep. Having asked the Deity, whither he
was to sail ? he was answered, " To the Gods : "
upon which he offered up a prayer for the good of
mankind. And he obeyed the divine admonition :
and built a vessel five stadia in length, and in breadth
two. Into this he put everything which he had got
ready ; and last of all conveyed into it his wife,
children, and friends. After the Flood had been
upon the earth, and was in time abated, Xisuthrus
sent out some birds[2] from the vessel, which, not
finding any food, nor any place to rest their feet,
returned to him again. After an interval of some
days, he sent them forth a second time, and they
now returned with their feet tinged with mud. He
made a trial a third time with these birds, but they
returned to him no more ; from whence he formed a
judgment, that the surface of the earth was now

---

[1] The sun was worshipped by the Assyrians as a God,
under the name of *Shamas*, the Hebrew *Shemesh*.

[2] Compare with Genesis viii. 7—12.

above the waters. Having, therefore, made an opening in the vessel, and finding, upon looking out, that the vessel was driven to the side of a mountain, he immediately quitted it, being attended by his wife, his daughter, and the pilot. Xisuthrus immediately paid his adoration to the earth, and, having constructed an altar, offered sacrifices[1] to the gods.

These things being duly performed, both Xisuthrus, and those who came out of the vessel with him, disappeared. They who remained in the vessel, finding that the others did not return, came out, with many lamentations, and called continually on the name of Xisuthrus. They saw him no more, but could distinguish his voice in the air, and could hear him admonish them to pay due regard to the gods. He likewise informed them that it was upon account of his piety that he was translated[2] to live with the gods ; that his wife and daughter, with the pilot, had obtained the same honour. To this he added that he would have them make the best of their way to Babylonia, and search for the writings at Sippara, which were to be made known to all mankind : and that the place where they then were was the land of Armenia.[3] The remainder having

---

[1] See Genesis viii. 20.

[2] Compare with this the translation of Enoch, Genesis v. 23, 24.

[3] Compare with Genesis viii. 4. Ararat is the Hebrew name of Armenia.—See 2 Kings xix. 37.

heard these words, offered sacrifices to the gods; and taking a circuit, journeyed towards Babylonia.

The vessel, being thus stranded in Armenia, some part of it yet remains in the Gordyæan[1] mountains in Armenia; and the people scrape off the bitumen,[2] with which it had been outwardly coated, and make use of it by way of an alexipharmic[3] and amulet. In this manner they returned to Babylon; and having found the writings at Sippara, they set about building cities, and erecting temples: and Babylon was thus inhabited again.—*Syncel. Chron.* 28.—*Euseb. Chron.* 5, 8.

## OF ABRAHAM.

After the Flood, in the tenth generation, there was a certain man among the Chaldeans, renowned for his justice and great exploits, and for his skill in the celestial sciences.—*Euseb. Praep. Evang.*, lib. ix.

## OF NABONASAR.

The Chaldeans, (from whom the Greek mathematicians copy,) are accurately acquainted with the motion of the stars only from the reign of Nabo-

---

[1] The mountains of Kurdistan.

[2] Or mineral pitch.—See Genesis vi. 14.

[3] *i.e.*, an antidote to poison, and an amulet, or charm, against the evil eye.

nasar. For Nabonasar collected all the chronicles of the kings prior to himself, and destroyed them, so that the enumeration of the Chaldean kings might commence with him.—From *Syncellus' Chronicon*, 207.

## OF THE DESTRUCTION OF THE JEWISH TEMPLE.

He (Nabopallasar) sent his son, Nabuchodonosor, (*i.e.*, Nebuchadnezzar) with a great army against Egypt, and against Judea, upon being informed that they had revolted from him ; and by that means he subdued them all, and set fire to the temple that was at Jerusalem, and removed our people[1] entirely out of their own country, and transferred them to Babylon ; and it happened that our city was desolate during the interval of seventy years, until the days of Cyrus king of Persia. (He then says, that), this Babylonian king conquered Egypt, and Syria, and Phœnicia, and Arabia, and exceeded in his exploits all that had reigned before him in Babylon and Chaldæa.—*Joseph contr. Apion.*, lib. 1, c. 19.

## OF NEBUCHADNEZZAR.

When Nabopollasar, his (Nebuchadnezzar's) father, heard that the governor, whom he had set over Egypt, and the parts of Cœlesyria and Phœnicia, had revolted, he was unable to put up with his

---

[1] The Jews.

delinquencies any longer, but committed certain parts of his army to his son, Nabuchodonosor (Nebuchadnezzar), who was then but young, and sent him against the rebel: and Nabuchodonosor fought with him, and conquered him, and reduced the country again under his dominion. And it happened that his father, Nabopollasar, fell into a distemper at this time, and died in the city of Babylon, after he had reigned twenty-nine years.

After a short time, Nabuchodonosor (Nebuchadnezzar), receiving the intelligence of his father's death, set the affairs of Egypt and the other countries in order, and committed the captives he had taken from the Jews and Phœnicians and Syrians, and of the nations belonging to Egypt, to some of his friends, in order that they might conduct that part of his forces that had on heavy armour, together with the rest of his baggage, to Babylonia; while he went in haste, with a few followers, across the desert to Babylon. When he was come there, he found that affairs had been well conducted by the Chaldeans, and that the principal person among them had preserved the kingdom for him. Accordingly, he now obtained possession of all his father's dominions. He ordered the captives to be distributed in colonies, in the most suitable places of Babylonia, and adorned the temple of Belus, with the other temples, in a sumptuous and pious manner, out of the spoils he had taken in this

F

war.   He also rebuilt the old city, (Babylon), and added another to it on the outside, and so far restored Babylon, that none who should besiege it afterwards might have it in their power to divert the river, so as to facilitate an entrance into it; and this he did by building three walls about the inner city, and three about the outer one.   Some of these walls he built of burnt brick, and bitumen, and some of brick only.  When he had thus admirably fortified the city with walls, and had magnificently adorned the gates, he added also a new palace to those in which his forefathers had dwelt, adjoining them, but exceeding them in height and in its great splendour. It would, perhaps, require too long a narration, if any one were to describe it; however, as prodigiously large and magnificent as it was, it was finished in fifteen days.   In this palace he erected very high walks, supported by stone pillars ; and by planting what was called a pensile paradise, and replenishing it with all sorts of trees, he rendered the prospect an exact resemblance of a mountainous country. This he did to please his queen,[1] because she had been brought up in Media, and was fond of a mountainous situation."—*Joseph contr. Apion.*, lib. I, c. 19.—*Syncel. Chron.* 220.—*Euseb. Præp. Evan.*, lib. 9.

---

[1] Amytis.

OF THE CHALDÆAN KINGS AFTER NEBUCHADNEZZAR.

" Nabuchodonosor, after he had begun to build the above-mentioned wall, fell sick, and departed this life, when he had reigned forty-three years; whereupon his son Evilmerodachus (Evilmerodach[1]— Jeremiah lii. 31) obtained the kingdom. He governed public affairs in an illegal and improper manner; and, by means of a plot laid against him by Neriglissoorus, (Neriglissor), his sister's husband, he was slain when he had reigned only two years. After his death, Neriglissor, who had conspired against him, succeeded him in the kingdom, and reigned four years. His son, Laborosoarchodus, obtained the kingdom, although a mere child, and reigned nine months. But, on account of the evil practices which he manifested, a plot being made against him by his friends, he was tortured to death.

After his death, the conspirators having assembled, by common consent, put the crown on the head of Nabonnedus,[2] a man of Babylon, one of the leaders of that insurrection. It was in his reign that the walls of Babylon were curiously built of burnt brick and bitumen.

In the seventeenth year of his, (Nabonidus's reign, Cyrus came out of Persia, with a great army,

---

[1] _i.c._ Man or servant of Merodach.　　[2] Nabonidus.

and having conquered all the rest of Asia, he came hastily to Babylonia. When Nabonnedus (Naboni-dus), perceived that he was advancing to attack him, he assembled his forces and opposed him, but was defeated, and fled with a few of his attendants, and was shut up in the city Borsippus. Whereupon Cyrus took Babylon, and gave orders that the outer walls should be demolished, because the city had proved very troublesome to him, and difficult to take. He then marched to Borsippus, to besiege Nabonnedus [Nabonidus]; but, as Nabonnedus de-livered himself into his hands without holding out the place, he was at first kindly treated by Cyrus, who gave him a habitation in Carmania, and sent him out of Babylonia. Accordingly, Nabonnedus [Nabonidus] spent the remainder of his time in that country, and there died."—*Joseph. contr. App.*, lib. I, c. 20.—*Euseb. Præp. Evan.*, lib. 10.

## OF THE FEAST OF SACEA.

"Berosus, in the first book of his Babylonian history, says: That in the eleventh month, called Lōos,[1] is celebrated in Babylon the Feast of Sacea, for five days; in which it is the custom that the masters should obey their domestics, one of whom is led round the house, clothed in a royal garment, and him they call Zoganes."—*Extracted from Athenæus*, lib. 14.

---

[1] The Macedonian month Lōos answers to our July.

CONCERNING THE INNOVATIONS INTRODUCED INTO THE
RELIGION OF THE PERSIANS BY ARTAXERXES II.

" They (the Persians) neither received images of
wood nor stone, as the Greeks ; nor worshipped
ibises and ichneumons, like the Egyptians ; but
only reverenced fire and water, like philosophers.

Berosus, however, relates in the 3rd Book of his
Chaldean Histories, that after many ages they
worshipped images in human form ; this being introduced by Artaxerxes, the son of Darius, the son
of Ochus, who having set up the image of Venus
Anaitis in Babylon, and Susa, and Ecbatana, Persia,
Bactria, Damascus, and Sardis, charged the people
to worship it."—Extracted from *Clement, Bishop of
Alexandria* (*Admonitio ad Gentes*), p. 43.

# CHRONOLOGICAL AND ASTRONOMICAL FRAGMENTS.

## OF THE GREAT YEAR.

" Berosus, who thus interprets the Babylonian tradition, says that these events take place according to the course of the stars ; and he affirms it so positively as to fix the time for the (general) conflagration of the world, and the Deluge. He maintains that all terrestrial things will be consumed when the planets, which now are traversing their different courses, shall all coincide in the sign of Cancer, and be so placed, that a straight line could pass directly through all their orbs. But the Flood will take place (he says) when the same conjunction of the planets shall take place in the constellation Capricorn. The summer is in the former constellation, the winter in the latter."—From *Seneca, Nat. Quæst.* iii., 29.

# MEGASTHENES:

## From Abydenus.

---

## Of Nebuchadnezzar.

"Abydenus, in his history of the Assyrians, has preserved the following fragment of Megasthenes, who says : That Nabucodrosorus [Nebuchadnezzar], having become more powerful than Hercules, invaded Libya and Iberia, [Spain], and·when he had rendered them tributary, he extended his conquests over the inhabitants of the shores upon the right of the sea.   It is, moreover, related by the Chaldæans, that as he went up into his palace he was possessed by some god ; and he cried out, and said : " Oh ! Babylonians, I, Nabucodrosorus (Nebuchadnezzar) foretel unto you a calamity which must shortly come to pass, which neither Belus my ancestor, nor his queen Beltis, have power to persuade the Fates to turn away.   A Persian mule shall come, and, by the assistance of your gods shall impose upon you the yoke of slavery ; the author of which shall be a Mede, the foolish pride of Assyria.   Before he should thus betray my subjects, Oh ! that some sea, or whirlpool, might receive him, and his memory be blotted out for ever ; or that he might be cast out to wander through some desert, where there are neither cities nor the trace of men ; a solitary exile among

rocks and caverns, where beasts and birds alone
abide. But for me, before he shall have conceived
these mischiefs in his mind, a happier end will be
provided." When he had thus prophesied, he
expired, and was succeeded by his son, Evilmaruchus
[Evilmerodach], who was slain by his kinsman,
Neriglisares [Neriglissor], and Neriglisares left a
son, Labassoarascus [Labarosoarchod]. And when
he also had suffered death by violence, they made
Nabannidochus[1] king, being of no relation to the
royal race. In his reign Cyrus [king of Persia]
took Babylon, and granted him a principality, [or
made him a satrap], in Karmania. Now, concerning
the rebuilding of Babylon by Nabuchodonosor,
he, [Megasthenes], writes thus : It is said that from
the beginning all things were water, called the sea
[Thalath] ; that Belus caused this state of things to
cease, and appointed to each its proper place, and
he [Belus] surrounded Babylon with a wall ; but in
process of time this wall disappeared, and Nabuchodonosor [Nebuchadnezzar] walled it in again,
and it remained so, with its brazen gates, until the
time of the Macedonian conquest, [i.e., by Alexander the Great], and after other things he says :
Nabuchodonosor having succeeded to the kingdom,
built the walls of Babylon in a triple circuit in fifteen
days ; and he turned the river Armacale,[2] a branch

---

[1] Nabonidus.

[2] Nahar Malcha, or Ar Malcha, i.e., the royal river, or canal.

of the Euphrates and the Acracanus; and above the
city of Sippara[1] he dug a receptacle for the waters,
whose perimeter was forty parasangs, and whose
depth was twenty cubits; and he placed gates at
the entrance thereof, by opening which they irrigated
the plains, and these they call Echetognomones
[sluices]; and he constructed dykes against the
irruptions of the Erythræan sea], the Persian Gulf]
and built the city of Teredon against the incursions
of the Arabs; and he adorned the palace with trees,
calling them hanging gardens.—*Euseb. Præb. Evan.*,
lib. 10.—*Euseb. Chron.* 49.

*End of the Fragments of Megasthenes.*

---

[1] *i.e.,* Sepharvaim.

## Of the Ark.

### From Nicolaus of Damascus, who lived about the time of Augustus Cæsar.

" There is above Minyas, in the land of Armenia, a very great mountain, which is called Baris[1] (*i.e.* a ship); to which it is said that many persons retreated at the time of the Flood, and were saved; and that one in particular was carried thither in an ark, and was landed on its summit; and that the remains of the vessel were long preserved upon the mountain. Perhaps this was the same individual of whom Moses, the legislator of the Jews, has made mention."— From *Josephus' Antiq. of the Jews*, Book i. 3. *Eusebius' Praep. Evang.*, 9.

## HESTIAEUS.

### Concerning the Dispersion of Mankind after the Flood. .

" The priests who escaped took with them the implements of the worship of the Enyalion Jove, and

---

[1] Epiphanius, one of the. Fathers, calls this mountain Lubar ; the Zend-Avesta styles it Al Bordj.

came to Senaar, in Babylonia. But they were again driven from thence by the introduction of a diversity of tongues, upon which they founded colonies in various parts, each settling in such situations as chance, or the direction of God, led them to occupy."
—*From Josephus' Antiq. of the Jews; and Eusebius' Preparatio Evangelica,* 9.


## ALEXANDER POLYHISTOR.

### CONCERNING THE TOWER OF BABEL.

" The Sibyl says, that when all men formerly spoke the same language, some among them undertook to erect a large and lofty tower, in order to climb into heaven. But God, (or the gods), sending forth a whirlwind, frustrated their design and gave to each tribe a particular language of its own, which (*confusion of tongues*) is the reason that the name of that city is called Babylon."

"After the Flood, Titan and Prometheus lived, and Titan undertook a war against Kronus."—Extracted from *Syncellus,* 44. *Josephus' Antiq. of Jews,* i. chap. 4.; *Euseb. Praep. Evang.,* 9.


## FROM THE SIBYLLINE ORACLES.

" But when the judgments of Almighty God
   Were ripe for execution ; when the tower
   Rose to the skies upon Assyria's plain,

And all mankind one language only knew :
A dread commission from on high was given
To the fell whirlwinds, which with dire alarms
Beat on the tower, and to its lowest base
Shook it convulsed.   And now all intercourse,
By some occult and overruling power,
Ceased among men.   By utterance they strove,
Perplexed and anxious, to disclose their mind,
But their lip failed them ; and in lieu of words
Produced a painful babbling sound : the place
Was thence called Babel ; by the apostate crew
Named from the event.   Then severed, far away
They sped, uncertain, into realms unknown :
Thus kingdoms rose, and the glad world was filled."

The Sibyl having named Kronus, Titan, and Iapetus (Japheth) as the three sons of the Patriarch (Noah), who governed the world in the tenth generation, after the Flood, and mentioned the division of the world into three parts, (viz, by *Shem, Ham, and Japheth*), over which each of the Patriarchs ruled in peace, then relates the death of Noah, and the war between Kronus and Titan.

N.B.—The translation given above is from Vol. IV. of *Bryant's Ancient Mythology*.   The fragment above given is mentioned by Josephus ; and some lines are quoted by the Christian Fathers, Athenagoras and Theophilus of Antioch.

## FROM EUPOLEMUS.

### Concerning the Tower of Babel, and Abraham.

"The City of Babylon owes its foundation to those who were saved from the catastrophe of the Flood ; these were the giants, (Heb. נְפִלִים = fallen ones), and they built the tower which is noticed in history. But the tower being overthrown by the interposition of God, the giants were scattered over all the earth.

He says, moreover, that in the tenth generation, in the City of Babylonia, called Camarina (which, by some, is called the city Urie, and which signifies a city of the Chaldeans), there lived, the thirteenth in descent, (a man named), Abraham, a man of a noble race and superior to all others in wisdom.

Of him they relate that he was the inventor of astrology and the Chaldean magic, and that on account of his eminent piety he was esteemed by God. It is further said, that under the directions of God he removed and lived in Phœnicia, and there taught the Phœnicians the motions of the sun and moon, and all other things ; for which reason he was held in great reverence by their king.[1]—Extracted from *Eusebius' Praep. Evan.*, 9.

---

[1] Abimelech, king of Gerar.

## FROM NICOLAS OF DAMASCUS.

### CONCERNING ABRAHAM.

"Abram was king of Damascus, and came thither as a stranger, with an army, from that part of the country which is situated above Babylon of the Chaldeans.    But after a short time he again emigrated from this region with his people, and transferred his dwelling to the land which was at that time called Canaaea, but is now called Judæa; together with all the multitude which had increased with him, of whose history I shall give an account in another book.    The name of Abram is well known even to this day in Damascus, and a village is pointed out which is still called the House of Abraham."— Extracted from *Eusebius, Praep. Evang.* 9, *and Josephus, Antiq. of the Jews,* i. 7.


## OF ABRAHAM AND HIS DESCENDANTS AND OF MOSES AND THE LAND OF ISRAEL.

FROM JUSTIN, OUT OF TROGUS POMPEIUS.   Book xviii. 3, 3, 5.   Book xxxvi. 2, 3, 6.

" The origin of the Jews was from Damascus, a most famous city of Syria, whence also the Assyrian kings, and queen Semiramis sprang.   The name of

the city was given it from king Damascus, in honour
of whom the Syrians consecrated the sepulchre of
his wife Arathis as a temple, and regard her as a
goddess worthy of the most sacred worship. After
Damascus, Azelus,[1] and then Adores, Abraham, and
Israhel were their kings. But a prosperous family
of ten sons made Israhel more famous than any of
his ancestors. Having divided his kingdom in consequence, into ten governments, he committed them
to his sons, and called the whole people Jews, from
Judas, who died soon after the division, and ordered
his memory to be held in veneration by them all, as
his portion was shared among them. The youngest
of the brothers was Joseph, whom the others, fearing
his extraordinary abilities, secretly made prisoner,
and sold to some foreign merchants. Being carried
by them into Egypt, and having there, by his great
powers of mind, made himself master of the arts of
magic, he found, in a short time, great favour with the
king; for he was eminently skilled in prodigies, and
was the first to establish the science of interpreting
dreams. And nothing, indeed, of divine, or human
law seems to have been unknown to him; so that he
foretold a famine or dearth in the land (*of Egypt*),
some years before it happened, and all Egypt would
have perished by famine, had not the king, by his
advice, ordered the corn to be laid up for several

---

[1] Hazael, King of Syria.

years : such being the proofs of his knowledge, that
his admonitions seemed to proceed, not from a
mortal, but a god.    His son was Moses, whom,
besides the inheritance of his father's knowledge, the
comeliness of his person also recommended.    But
the Egyptians, being troubled with scabies and
leprosy, and moved by some oracular prediction,
expelled him, with those who had the disease, out of
Egypt, that the distemper might not spread among
a greater number.    Becoming leader, accordingly, of
the exiles, he carried off by stealth the sacred utensils
of the Egyptians, who, endeavouring to recover them
by force of arms, were obliged by tempests to return
home ; and Moses, having reached Damascus, the
birth-place of his fore-fathers, took possession of
Mount Sinai ; on his arrival at which, after having
suffered, together with his followers, from a seven
days' fast in the deserts of Arabia, he consecrated
every seventh day, (according to the present custom
of the nation), for a fast-day, and to be perpetually
called a Sabbath, because that day had ended at once
their hunger and their wanderings.    And, as they
remembered that they had been driven from Egypt
for fear of spreading infection, they took care, in
order that they might not become odious, from the
same cause, to the inhabitants of the country, to have
no communication with strangers; a rule which, from
having been adopted on that particular occasion,
gradually became a custom and part of their religion.

After the death of Moses, his son Aruas[1] was made
priest for celebrating the rites which they brought
from Egypt, and soon after created king; and ever
afterwards, it was a custom among the Jews to have
the same chiefs both for kings and priests; and, by
uniting religion with the administration of justice,
it is almost incredible how powerful they became.
The wealth of the (*Jewish*) nation was augmented
by the duties on balm, (balsam), which is produced
only in that country; for there is a valley, encircled
with an unbroken ridge of hills, as it were a wall
in the form of a camp, the space enclosed being
about 200 acres, and called by the name of Hieri-
chus, (Jericho); in which valley there is a wood,
remarkable both for its fertility and pleasant-
ness, and chequered with groves of palm and
balm-trees. The balm-trees resemble pitch-trees[2] in
shape, except that they are not so tall, and are
dressed after the manner of vines; and at a certain
season of the year they exude the balm. But the
place is not less admired for the genial warmth
of the sun in it, than for its fertility; for, though the
sun in that climate is the hottest in the world, there
is constantly in this valley a certain natural subdued
tepidity in the air. In this country also is the lake
Asphaltites, which, from its magnitude and the

---

[1] Aaron.  [2] Pitch-pine.

stillness of its waters, is called the Dead Sea ; for, it is neither agitated by the winds, because the bituminous matter, with which all its water is clogged, resists even hurricanes ; nor does it admit of navigation, for all inanimate substances sink to the bottom; and it will support no wood, except such as is smeared with alum."—*Extracted from the Philippine History of Justin, the Abbreviator of Trogus Pompeius.*

## CONCERNING BELUS.

### FROM EUPOLEMUS.

" For the Babylonians say that the first was Belus, who is the same as Kronus. And from him descended Belus and Chanaan ; and this Chanaan was the father of the Phœnicians.

" Another of his sons was Khum, (*i.e.*, Ham), who is called by the Greeks Asbolus, the father of the Ethiopians, and the brother of Mestraim,[1] the father of the Egyptians. The Greeks say, moreover, that Atlas was the discoverer of astrology."—*Extracted from Eusebius, Praep. Evang.*, Book ix.

### FROM THALLUS.

" Thallus makes mention of Belus, the King of the Assyrians, and Kronus, (Saturn) the Titan, and says,

---

[1] Mizraim.

that Belus, with the Titans, made war against Zeus, (Jupiter) and his compeers, who are called gods. He says, moreover, that Gygus was smitten, and fled to Tartessus (in Spain).

"According to the history of Thallus, Belus preceded the Trojan war 322 years."—*From Theophylact ad Autolycus*, 281-2.


## OF THE ASSYRIAN EMPIRE.

### FROM KTESIAS.

"In like manner, all the other kings succeeded, the son receiving the empire from his father, being altogether thirty in their generations to Sardanapalus. In his time the empire passed to the Medes from the Assyrians, having remained with them upwards of 1,360 years, according to the account of Ktesias the Cnidian, in his second book."—*Extracted from Diodorus Siculus*, Book ii. p. 77.


### FROM DIODORUS SICULUS.

"In the manner above related, the empire of the Assyrians, after having continued from Ninus thirty generations, and more than 1,400 years, was finally dissolved by the Medes."—*Extracted from Diodorus Siculus*, Book ii. p. 81.

## FROM HERODOTUS.

"The Medes were the first who began the revolt from the Assyrians, after they had maintained the dominion over Upper Asia for a period of 520 years."—Extracted from *Herodotus*, Book i. ch. 95.

## OF NABOPOLLASAR.

### FROM ALEXANDER POLYHISTOR.

"Nabopollasar, (whom Alexander Polyhistor calls Sardanapallus), sent to Astyages, the satrap of Media, and demanded his daughter, Amuïtes,[1] in marriage for his son, Nabuchodonosor [Nebuchadnezzar]. He was the commander of the army of Saracus, King of the Chaldeans, and, having been sent upon some expedition, turned his arms against Saracus, and marched against the city of Ninus (Nineveh). But Saracus, confused by his approach, set fire to his palace, and burnt himself in it. And Nabopollasar obtained the empire of the Chaldeans. He was the father of Nabuchodonosor" [Nebuchadnezzar].— From *Eusebius' Chronicon*, 46.

---

[1] Amytis.

## OF THE CHALDEAN AND ASSYRIAN KINGS.

### FROM ALEXANDER POLYHISTOR.

"In addition to the above, Polyhistor continues thus: After the deluge, says he, Evexius held possession of the country of the Chaldeans during a period of four neri. And he was succeeded by his son, Comosbelus, who held the empire four neri and five sossi. But, from the time of Xisuthrus[1] and the Flood, to that period at which the Medes took possession of Babylon, there were altogether 86 kings. Polyhistor enumerates and mentions each of them by name, from the volume of Berossus; the duration of the reigns of all which kings comprehends a period of 33,091 years. But, when their power was thus firmly established, the Medes suddenly levied forces against Babylon to surprise it, and to place upon the throne kings chosen from among themselves. He, (Polyhistor), then gives the names of the Median kings, eight in number, who reigned during the period of 224 years; and, again, eleven kings during . . . . [2] years. Then 49 kings of the Chaldeans, 458 years. Then nine kings of the Arabians, 245 years. After all these successive periods of years, he states that Semiramis reigned over the Assyrians. And again he minutely enumerates the names of 45 kings, assigning to them a term of 526 years. After whom,

---

[1] Khasis-Adra.   [2] No number is given in the original text.

he says, there was a king of the Chaldeans whose name was Phulus, of whom also the historical writings of the Hebrews make mention under the name of Phulus (Pul), who, they say, invaded the country of the Jews."—*Extracted from the Armenian Chronicon of Eusebius*, 39.

## OF SENNACHERIB.

### FROM ALEXANDER POLYHISTOR.

"After the reign of the brother of Senecherib, Akises reigned over the Babylonians ; and, when he had governed for the space of 30 days, he was slain by Marodach Baladanus, who held the empire by force during six months ; and he was slain, and succeeded by a person named Elibus.[1] But, in the 3rd year of his reign, Senecherib, king of the Assyrians, levied an army against the Babylonians ; and, in a battle in which they were engaged, conquered him and took him prisoner, with his adherents, and commanded them to be carried off into the land of the Assyrians. Having taken upon himself the government of the Babylonians, he appointed his son Assordanius,[2] their king, and he, (Sennacherib), again retired into Assyria.

" When he received a report that the Greeks had made a hostile descent upon Cilicia, he marched

---

[1] Belibus, in the Annals of Sennacherib, of the Bellino Cylinder. (See *Records of the Past*, vol. i., p. 26.)

[2] Esarhaddon.

against them, and fought with them a pitched battle; in which, though he suffered great loss in his own army, he overthrew them, and upon the spot he erected the statue of himself as a monument of his victory; and ordered his prowess to be inscribed upon it in the Chaldæan characters, to hand down the remembrance of it to posterity. He built also the city of Tarsus; after the likeness of Babylon, which he called Tharsis. And, after enumerating the various exploits of Sinnecherim, (Sennacherib), he adds that he reigned 18 years, and was cut off by a conspiracy, which had been formed against his life by his son Ardu-Musanus."—*Extracted from Eusebius, Armen. Chron.,* 42.


## OF SENNACHERIB AND HIS SUCCESSORS.

### FROM ALEXANDER POLYHISTOR.

" And after him (Pul), according to Polyhistor, Senecherib was king.

[The Chaldæan historian also makes mention of Senecherib himself, and Asordanus (Esarhaddon) his son, and Marodach Baladanus, as well as Nabuchodonosorus.][1]

" And Sinecherim (Sennacherib) reigned 18 years; and after him his son (Esarhaddon) reigned eight years. Then Sammuges (Saulmugina ?) reigned 21

---

[1] These remarks, within brackets, are by Eusebius.

years, and likewise his brother 21 years. Then Nabupalsar, (Nabopollassar), reigned 20 years; and after him Nabucodrossorus, (Nebuchadnezzar), reigned 43 years.

Therefore, from Sinecherim to Nabucodrossorus is comprehended a period altogether of 88 years. After Samuges, Sardanapallus[1] the Chaldean, reigned 21 years. He sent an army to the assistance of Astyages the Mede, Prince and Satrap of the family, that he might give Amunhean,[2] the daughter of Astyages, to his son Nabucodrossorus (Nebuchadnezzar). Then Nabucodrossorus reigned 43 years, and he came with a mighty army, and led the Jews, and Phœnicians, and Syrians into captivity. And after Nabucodrossorus, his son, Amilmarudochus, (Evil-Merodach—man, *i.e.*, Servant of Merodach), reigned 12 years.

And after him, Neglisarus (Neriglissor), reigned over the Chaldaeans 4 years; and then Nabodenus, (Nabonidus), reigned 17 years. In his reign, Cyrus, the son of Cambyses, invaded the country of the Babylonians. Nabodenus, (Nabonidus), went out to give him battle, but was defeated, and betook himself to flight; and Cyrus reigned at Babylon 9 years. He was killed, however, in another battle, which took place in the plain of Daas. After him Cambyses

---

[1] Nabopollasar, see p. 84.          [2] Amytis.

reigned 8 years; then Darius 36 years; and after him, Xerxes, and the other kings of the Persian line."
—*Extracted from Euseb. Armen. Chron.*, pp. 41, 42, 44, 45.

## OF SENNACHERIB AND HIS SUCCESSORS.

### FROM ABYDENUS.

"At the same time, the twenty-fifth, who was Senecherib, can hardly be recognized among the kings. It was he who subjected the city of Babylon to his power, and defeated and sunk a Grecian fleet upon the coast of Cilicia. He built also a temple at Athens, and erected brazen statues, upon which he engraved his own exploits. And he built the city of Tarsus, after the plan and likeness of Babylon, that the river Cydnus should flow through Tarsus, in the same manner as the Euphrates intersected Babylon. Next in order after him reigned Nergilus (Neriglissor?), who was assassinated by his son Adramelus, (Adrammelech?) and he also was slain by Axerdes (Sharezer?), his brother by the same father but of a different mother, who pursued his army, and shut it up in the city of Byzantium, (*lit.*, of the Byzantines). Axerdes was the first that levied mercenary soldiers, one of whom was Pythagoras, a follower of the wisdom of the Chaldeans; he also reduced under his dominion Egypt, and the country of Coele-Syria, from whence came Sardanapallus.[1]

" After him, Saracus reigned over the Assyrians; and when he was informed that a very great multitude of barbarians had come up from the sea to attack him, he sent Busalossorus, as his general, in haste to Babylon. But he, having with a treasonable design obtained Amuhean, [Amytis], the daughter of Astyages, the prince of the Medes, to be affianced to his son Nabuchodrossorus, (Nebuchadnezzar), marched straightway to surprise the city of Ninus, *i.e.*, Nineveh.

" But, when Saracus, the king, was apprized of all these proceedings, he burnt the royal palace.[2] And Nabuchodrossorus, (Nebuchadnezzar), succeeded to the empire, and surrounded Babylon with a strong wall."—*Extracted from Euseb. Arm. Chron.* 53.

## OF BELUS AND THE ASSYRIAN EMPIRE.

### From Castor.

" Belus, says Castor, was king of the Assyrians; and, under him, the Cyclops assisted Jupiter with thunderbolts and lightnings, in his contest with the Titans. At that time there were kings of the

---

[1] The name Sardanapalus being applied to various persons leaves it doubtful whether Saracus or Busalossorus, (*i.e.*, Nabopollassar), be intended.

[2] *Or*, entrusted the palace to Egoritus. Doubtful in the original, according to the Armenian editor.

Titans, one of whom was Ogygus. (After a short digression he proceeds to say,) that the giants, in their attempted inroads upon the gods, were slain by the assistance of Hercules and Dionysus,[1] who were themselves of the Titan race. Belus, whom we have mentioned above, was, after his death, esteemed a god. After him, Ninus reigned over the Assyrians 52 years. He married Semiramis, who, after his decease, reigned over the Assyrians 42 years. Then Zames, (who is the same as Ninyas,) reigned. (Then he enumerates each of the successive kings in order, and mentions them all, down to Sardanapallus, by their respective names : whose names, and the length of their reigns, we shall also give presently. Castor mentions them in his Canon in the following words) : ' We have first digested into a Canon the kings of the Assyrians, commencing with Belus : but, since we have no certain tradition respecting the length of his reign, we have merely set down his name, and commenced the chronological series from Ninus ; and have concluded it with another Ninus, who obtained the empire after Sardanapallus ; that, in this manner, the whole length of the time, as well as of the reign of each king, might be plainly set forth. Thus, it will be found, that the complete sum

---

[1] Dionysus is the Greek name for Bacchus. It is of Assyrian origin, being properly דִין נִיסִי DAYAN-NISI, *i.e.*, *Judge of Men*, or *Ruler of Men*, a title of the Sun, (Shamas) as a deity.

of the years amounts to 1280.'"—Extracted from *Euseb. Arm. Chron.*, p. 81.

### FROM DAMASCIUS.

" But the Babylonians, like the rest of the Barbarians, pass over in silence the One principle of the universe, and they constitute two, Tauthe and Apason, making Apason the husband of Tauthe, and denominating her the 'mother of the gods.' And, from these proceeds an only-begotten son, Moymis, which, I conceive, is no other than the intelligible world proceeding from the two principles. From them, also, another progeny is derived, Dache and Dachus; and again a third, Kissare and Assorus, from which last three others proceed, Anus and Illinus, and Aus. And of Aus and Davke is born a son called Belus, who, they say, is the fabricator of the world—the Demiurgus."[1]

### FROM AGATHIAS.

" But Jupiter they call Belus, and Hercules they they call Sandes,[2] and Venus Anaitis, and the rest they call differently; as Berosus the Babylonian, and Athenocles and Simacos, among others who have written the antiquities of the Assyrians and Medes, have related."—*De rebus gestis Justiniani, ed. Bonaventuræ, Parisiis*, 1650.

---

[1] For illustration and explanation of this fragment see *The Chaldacan Account of Genesis*, pp. 64, 66.

[2] Samdan in Assyrian.

# THE FRAGMENTS

OF

# THE EGYPTIAN HISTORIES:

CONTAINING

## THE OLD CHRONICLE;

## THE REMAINS OF MANETHO;

AND

## THE LATERCULUS OF ERATOSTHENES.

# INTRODUCTION.

## ABYDENUS

Was a Greek writer, contemporary with, and disciple of Berosus, the Chaldean, about B.C. 268. He wrote a history of the Chaldean empire, fragments of which are preserved to us in the writings of Eusebius, Cyrillus, and Syncellus. Some regard him as the same person as Palaephatus, who was also an Abydenus, *i.e.*, a native of the city Abydus.

## MEGASTHENES,

A Greek historian and geographer, who was sent by Seleucus Nicator as ambassador to India, about 295 B.C. On his return he wrote a book on India, which has unfortunately perished, with the exception of such fragments as are preserved in the works of Strabo, Josephus, and Arrian. The fragments of the *Indica* have been collected and published by *Schwanbeck*, with notes and explanations (*Bonn*, 1846). They are also to be found, with a Latin translation, in *Müller's Fragmenta Graeca*.

# ERATOSTHENES

Was an African by birth, the pride of Cyrene, as Strabo calls him. He reduced two sciences, which he found in their infancy, to a system—geography and chronology. He was born about 276 B.C., and held, under Euergetes, king of Egypt, the honourable post of Director of the Alexandrian Library. His researches into Egyptian history and chronology were undertaken by command of the King, and, consequently, with every advantage that royal patronage could procure. They were more especially devoted to the " so-called Theban kings," and were completed and edited by Apollodorus, the chronographer.

---

# APOLLODORUS,

To whom we are indebted for the preservation of some of these precious fragments, was a native of Athens, the son of Asclepiades, and pupil of Aristarchus. He flourished about B.C. 140, and continued the chronological researches of Eratosthenes of Cyrene. He is styled "the chronographer, Apollodorus," by Clement, Bishop of Alexandria, and, by Diodorus Siculus, he is distinguished as "Apollodorus, who treats of the computation of time." He wrote, besides his mythological work called the *Bibliotheca*—of which we possess three entire books—a chronicle in iambic verse, comprising a period of 1040 years from the Trojan war down to his own time. He was, in fact, both a chronographer and grammarian by profession. Eratosthenes was the founder of chronology and geography; and Apollodorus, having taken up the interrupted researches of Eratosthenes, became the publisher and continuator of his work.

## JULIUS AFRICANUS.

Julius Africanus, or the African, was Bishop of Emmaus [Nicopolis], in Judæa, at the beginning of the third century. He is regarded as the first editor of the Lists of Manetho, and is said to have compiled a chronological work, in five books, all of which, excepting only a few fragments, have unfortunately perished.

These precious relics have been collected and admirably arranged by Routh, in his *Reliquiæ Sacræ*, vol. iii. They exhibit throughout the man of judgment, integrity, and information; zealous in collecting and examining the oldest Chaldean and Egyptian records, especially those of Berosus and Manetho.

G

As he did not attempt the arrangement of a system of Annals with a regular notation of synchronisms, he gave the traditions unadulterated, just as he found them, contenting himself with proving from their own internal evidence the extravagance of those myriads of years admitted in the computation of his Pagan opponents.

He would seem, however, to have attempted the formation of a scheme of dates, according to the scriptural years of the world, with incidental notations of synchronisms, in order to bring the Bible-history into a certain connection with the Greek chronology. We know from Syncellus and a fragment of Africanus himself, that he assumed the year of the world 5500, (which we, following the Hebrew text, according to Archbishop Usher, make 4004), to be that of the Incarnation of Jesus Christ.

This assumption, which upon his authority has remained a standard dogma with the Fathers of the Greek Church, is, in truth, far preferable to the calculations of the Western Churches and those of Sir Isaac Newton; it rests, however, upon wholly conjectural grounds.

According to Africanus, following the Septuagint computation,—

| | A.M. |
|---|---|
| The Flood occurred    -    -    -    - | 2262 |
| The Birth of Abraham-    -    -    - | 2302 |
| Joseph's Death   -    -    -    -    - | 3563 |
| The Exodus of the Israelites from Egypt | 3705 |

|  |  | A.M. |
|---|---|---|
| Building of Solomon's Temple | - - | 4457 |
| First Olympiad after the Exodus 1020 - | | 4725 |
| (Contemporaneous with Jotham, King of Judah). | | |
| Beginning of the Reign of Cyrus, King of Persia - - - - - - | | 4942 |
| (In the first year of the 55th Olympiad). | | |
| The Birth of Christ | - - - - | 5500 |

From this table we see that Africanus, in the disputed dates, adheres to the Alexandrian tradition; he, consequently, assumes 215 years for the sojourn of the Israelites in Egypt.

But neither the Bible, nor Josephus, affords the least explanation of the 744 years assigned by him as the period between the Exodus and the building of the Temple. We must, however, take into consideration that, it is with him a settled thing, that the period from the Flood of Ogyges and the reign of Phoroneus to the first Olympiad was 1020 years. He assigns this same period for the interval between Moses and Solomon; and agrees with Josephus in admitting 25 years for Joshua. Africanus fortifies himself in this delusion on the subject of Greek synchronisms by two totally inadmissible assumptions. First, by a statement of Polemus, that in the time of Apis, son of Phoroneus, a portion of the Egyptian army left their own country, and established themselves in Palestine; and, secondly, by a statement in the text of Apion, (resting upon no

better authority than that of Ptolemy the Mendesian), to the effect that, in the time of Inachus,[1]
under the reign of Amōs, Moses led the Israelites
out of Egypt. This gives us a key to his asser-
tion in this version of the Lists of Manetho, that
Moses withdrew from Egypt under Amōs, the chief
of the 18th dynasty. But, the above statement of
Ptolemy the Mendesian rests solely on the assumption that Amōs destroyed Avaris, the stronghold of
the Hyk-sos, or Shepherd-Kings. Admitting this,
the only conclusion to be drawn from it would be,
that the expulsion of the Hyk-sos from all Egypt
was ascribed to Amōs. From the notices, however,
contained in Manetho's historical work, we learn,
that it was the so-called Mephra-Tuthmōsis, (whose
reign cannot be placed earlier than *fifth* in the list
of the 18th dynasty), who occupied Avaris after his
convention with the Hyk-sos. It is, however,
altogether nugatory to confound the Exodus with
the expulsion of the Hyk-sos. That they were
even contemporary events seems irreconcilable with
any traces of historical truth in the Book of Exodus.
The fatal love of synchronisms exercised an evil
influence upon the worthy Africanus, and thus prevented any close examination of Manetho's account.
—Abridged and adapted from Bunsen's *Egypt's
Place in History*, pp. 212—217.

---

[1] The first king of Argos, B.C. 1910.

## ALEXANDER POLYHISTOR.

This writer was born in Ionia or Phrygia, and was a pupil of the grammarian Krates. On account of his great fame as a scholar he obtained the epithet of Polyhistor. Captured in the war which the Romans waged against Mithridates, king of Pontus, he was bought by Cornelius Lentulus, who made him tutor to his sons. He received from his master the cognomen of Cornelius, (a custom then in use among the Romans); and, as a freed-man, became known as Alexander Cornelius Polyhistor. He lived at Rome in the time of the dictator Sylla, that is about 85 B.C., and perished in the flames by which the house of Lentulus was destroyed. He was a voluminous writer, but unfortunately his works have all perished. We are chiefly indebted to the Byzantine writer, Suidas, for what little we know of Polyhistor. Stephen of Byzantium, (*De Urbibus et Populis*), says that Polyhistor was a native of Cotiaei, a city of Phrygia, that he was either a son, or a disciple of Asclepiades, and that he wrote forty-two books on all kinds of subjects.

Clemens of Alexandria[1] quotes from the first book of a work, "*Concerning the Jews;*" and Eusebius

---

[1] *Clemens Alex. Stromata*, p. 332, ed Sylburg.

also, speaks of him with the highest praise.[1]
Richter[2] says it cannot be doubted that Pliny is
greatly indebted to him for much that he relates in
his Natural History. (Vide Pliny, *Historia Nat.* iii.
21, vii. 49, ix. 56, xiii. 39, xvi. 6, xxxvi. 17, edit.
Harduin.)

Plutarch and Photius, (cod. 188), have also mentioned Polyhistor; but we have no proof that Polyhistor had himself read the books of Berosus the
Chaldæan, because he appeals to Apollodorus in
reference to subjects related by the former.

# SYNCELLUS.

George the Syncellus, (*i.e.* the cell-companion), of
the Greek Patriarch of Constantinople, (Byzantium),
was born about A.D. 800. He is the author of a
chronography, which extends from the Creation of
the world down to A.D. 284. His work rests chiefly
upon the authority of Julius Africanus and Eusebius,
both of whom he accuses of serious errors. To this
work—continued down to A.D. 813, by Theophanes
the Isaurian—we are indebted for several fragments

---

[1] Eusebius, in his *Praeparatio Evangelica.* Book ix. 17.
[2] In his *Berosi Chaldæorum Historiæ quæ supersunt,*
p. 33. Leipsig, 1825.

of Berosus, Manetho, and other writers whose works have long since perished.

Further information concerning these writers— Apollodorus, Eratosthenes, Manetho, Julius Africanus, and Syncellus—with a critical estimate of the value of their respective systems of chronology, will be found in the learned work of Baron Bunsen, *Egypt's Place in Universal History*, vol. i., to which I am greatly indebted.

# INTRODUCTION TO THE LISTS OF MANĔTHO.

BEFORE the æra of the Ptolemies no native work was accessible to the Greeks, either on the doctrine, the chronology, or the history of Egypt. Manĕtho, an Egyptian priest, of Sebennytus, undertook to supply the deficiency in regard to each of these branches, and thereby formed an epoch in the researches of the Greeks, and of the Egyptians themselves. His historical work comprised a period of 3,555 years, from Menes, the first human monarch of Egypt, down to Alexander the Great. "The period," says Syncellus, "of the hundred and thirteen generations, described by Manĕtho in his three volumes, comprises a sum total of three thousand five hundred and fifty-five years;" that is, from the time of Menes to the death of the younger Nectanebo, the last of the native kings of Egypt. Of this period, thirteen centuries belonged to the Old Empire, nine to the Middle, and thirteen to the New. Manĕtho, whose Egyptian name was clearly Manĕthoth—*i.e.*, Ma-n-thoth—"he who was given by Thoth," (the Mercury or Hermes of the Egyptians,) is known to ancient authors as a priest of Sebennytus, living in high estimation at the court of the first Ptolemy, the son of Lagus, surnamed Soter. It is probable that Manĕtho also lived under Ptolemy Philadelphus II., since the authors of the *Apotelesmata*, and the Book of Sothis, or the Dog-star, who usurped his name, dedicated their forgery to that king.

Manĕtho, the Egyptian scholar and priest, evidently owes his high reputation to the merit of being the first who distinguished himself as a writer and critic upon religion and philosophy, as well as chronology and history ; using the Greek language, but drawing his materials from native sources, especially the Sacred Books of his nation. "Manĕtho, the Egyptian," says Eusebius, "not only reduced the whole Egyptian history into a Greek form, but also their entire system of theology, in his treatise, entitled ' The Sacred Book,' as well as in other works."

Theodoret, Bishop of Cyrus,[1] in the second quarter of the fifth century, describes Manĕtho (Sermon ii. de Therapeut), as "the author of a mythological work, or works, concerning Isis and Osiris, Apis and Serapis, and the other Egyptian deities." Manĕtho is also quoted by Plutarch, Ælian, Diogenes Laertius, and Suidas. This distinguished historian, sage, and scholar—the man whom all our ancient authorities mention with respect, is become almost a mythological personage ; and his works, with the exception of a few fragments, have been swept away by the destructive hand of time. What the school of Aristotle had prepared, and Manĕtho, under Greek

---

[1] *Or* Cyropolis, in Syria, a city built by the Jews in honour of, and in gratitude to, Cyrus, as the liberator of their nation from Babylonian servitude.

auspices, but with Egyptian learning, had matured,
Eratosthenes of Cyrene, and Apollodorus of Athens
carried to perfection ; so that, by their efforts, the
chronology of Egypt became the common property
of mankind.    Unfortunately, nothing remains of the
labours of Apollodorus except the number of kings
for the middle Empire ; while Eratosthenes's register
of the earlier Pharaohs has reached us only in a
meagre epitome.    To George Syncellus of Byzantium, (Constantinople), we are indebted for an extract
from a work of Eratosthenes devoted to the subject
of Egyptian chronology, which he introduces with
the following prefatory remarks :—" Apollodorus,
the chronographer, has described another dynasty of
Egyptian kings, called Thebans, thirty-eight in number, whose united reigns comprised 1,076 years.
This succession extends from the year of the world,
2900 (or, according to Syncellus, from the 124th
year after the Confusion of Tongues), to the year
3975.    Eratosthenes, (as stated by Apollodorus),
compiled his notices of these kings from Egyptian
monuments and lists, by order of the King, and
arranged their names—each with its Greek translation—in the following order." Then follows a List of
Kings beginning with Menes—every Egyptian name
with its Greek translation annexed.    The number of
years for each reign is also subjoined.    Thus we
have a list of Egyptian kings, drawn up by Eratosthenes, and edited by Apollodorus, the chrono-

grapher; beginning with Menes, and containing thirty-eight reigns in 1,076 years—the editor himself added to it another list of fifty-three kings, in continuity of succession. But, having, like Josephus, and all the Christian chronographers, placed Moses and the Exodus at the beginning of the eighteenth dynasty, what, then, was to be done with the other fifty-three kings who reigned before the eighteenth dynasty? It is, then, to this circumstance that we are indebted for the copious extracts from Manetho's historical work of the names of the kings of that dynasty. Eratosthenes began his labours with Menes, and, no doubt, concluded them with some notable epoch—some important historical crisis. This event was unquestionably the invasion of the Shepherds, and the occupation of the Egyptian throne by the Shepherd-kings, (the Hyk-sos); for the whole history of Egypt turned upon this event, as proved by the monuments and attested by Manetho.

Eratosthenes, therefore, must be our guide for the chronology of the Old Empire, so long as his data are in harmony with those derived from the monuments. The Old Empire terminated with the third king of the thirteenth dynasty; the occupation of the throne of Memphis by the Shepherd-kings was the commencement of the Middle Empire, and their expulsion that of the New. For the Middle Empire we must follow Apollodorus of Athens, for, if the lists of kings furnished by Eratosthenes embraced

the Old Empire, Apollodorus must have commenced
with the Middle Empire, for his fifty-three kings
follow immediately upon those of Eratosthenes. Nor
can there be any reasonable doubt as to the extent
of the period they occupied. Syncellus did not deign
to transcribe their names, because they appeared to
him utterly useless. The names of the kings of the
eighteenth Dynasty consequently were *not* among
them, for he was not only well acquainted with those,
but considered them of the greatest importance.
Syncellus subjected this Dynasty, (the eighteenth,) to
a very careful analysis, because the birth of Moses
and the Exodus were connected with it. The
labours of Apollodorus did not, therefore, extend to
the New Empire. Such an hypothesis were indeed,
as Bunsen remarks, hardly in itself admissible, for
Manetho assigns, at most, fifty-seven Theban kings
of the thirteenth Dynasty to this period, and those
of Apollodorus are also expressly called Thebans.
Lastly, the correspondence between the number fifty-
three in Apollodorus, and fifty-seven in Manetho,
were as close as could reasonably be expected or
desired as an argument in favour of their identity of
period. Everything, therefore, combines, as Bunsen states, to show the probability of our having
discovered the true system of Eratosthenes and
Apollodorus, and with it a key to the right understanding of the Lists of Manĕtho.—*Bunsen's Egypt's
Place in History*, 142-144, *et passim*.

# MANETHO.

" It remains, therefore, to make certain extracts concerning the dynasties of the Egyptians, from the writings of Manetho, the Sebennyte, the high-priest of the idolatrous temples of Egypt, in the time of Ptolemaeus Philadelphus. These, according to his own account, he copied from the inscriptions which were engraved, in the sacred dialect and hierographic characters, upon the columns set up in the Seriadic land by Thoth, the first Hermes, (Mercury); and after the Flood, were translated from the sacred dialect into the Greek tongue, in hieroglyphic characters, and committed to writing in books, and deposited by Agathodæmon, the son of the second Hermes, the father of Tat, (Taut of the Phœnician mythology), in the penetralia of the temples of Egypt. He has addressed and explained them to Philadelphus, the second king (of Egypt) who bore the name of Ptolemaeus, in the book which he has entitled Sothis, (or the Dog-star)." This epistle is as follows :—

## THE EPISTLE OF MANETHO,[1] THE SEBENNYTE, TO PTOLEMY PHILADELPHUS.

" To the great and august King, Ptolemy Philadelphus : Manetho, the High-priest and Scribe of the

---

[1] This Epistle is now generally regarded as that of the pseudo-Manetho ; not the Manetho who wrote the lists of kings, but one who assumed and abused his name.

sacred adyta in Egypt, being by birth a Sebennyte and a citizen of Heliopolis, to his sovereign Ptolemy, humbly greeting :

" It is right for us, most mighty King, to pay due attention to all things which it is your pleasure we should take into consideration.   In answer, then, to your inquiries concerning the things which shall come to pass in the world, I shall, according to your commands, lay before you what I have gathered from the sacred books written by Hermes Trismegistus, our forefather.   Farewell, my Prince and Sovereign."—*Syncel. Chron.* 40.—*Euseb. Chron.*

# MANĔTHO.

## THE EGYPTIAN DYNASTIES.

### The Dynasty of the Demigods.

The 1st of the Egyptian kings was Hephæstus, (Vulcan), who reigned 724 and a half years and four days.

The 2nd was Helios (*i.e.* the Sun), the son of Hephæstus (*who reigned*) 86 years.

3rd, Agathodæmon, who reigned 56 and a half years and ten days.

4th, Kronus (Saturn) 40 and a half years.

5th, Osiris and Isis, 35 years.

6th, . . . years.

7th, Typhon, 29 years.

8th, Horus, the demigod, 25 years.

6th, Ares (Mars), the demigod, 23 years.

10th, Anubis, the demigod, 17 years.

11th, Heracles (*i.e.* Hercules) the demigod, 15 years.

12th, Apollo, the demigod, 25 years.

13th, Ammon, the demigod, 30 years.

14th, Tithoes, the demigod, 27 years.

15th, Sosus, the demigod, 32 years.

16th, Zeus, [*i.e.*, Jupiter], the demigod, 20 years.— *Syncel. Chron.* 19.—*Euseb. Chron.* 7.

## THE EGYPTIAN DYNASTIES AFTER THE DELUGE.

### The First Dynasty.

1. After the dead demigods, the first dynasty consisted of eight kings, of whom the first was Mēnes the Thinite ; he reigned 62 years, and perished by a wound received from a hippopotamus.

2. Athōthis, his son, reigned 57 years ; he built the palaces at Memphis, and left the anatomical books, for he was a physician.

3. Kenkenēs, his son, reigned 31 years.

4. Venephes, his son, reigned 23 years. In his time a great plague raged through Egypt. He erected the pyramids near Cochome.

5. Usaphædus, his son, reigned 20 years.

6. Miebidus, his son, reigned 26 years.

7. Semempsis, his son, reigned 18 years. In his reign a terrible pestilence afflicted Egypt.

8. Biēnechēs, his son, reigned 26 years.

The whole number of years amounted to 253 [or 263, according to the true reckoning].

### The Second Dynasty

Consisted of nine Thinite kings.

1. Boëthus the First reigned 38 years. During his reign a chasm of the earth opened near Bubastus, and many persons perished.

2. Kaeachōs reigned 39 years. Under him the

bulls, Apis in Memphis, and Meneus, (Mnēvis), in Heliopolis, and the Mendēsian goat, were appointed to be gods.

3. Binōthris reigned 47 years. In his time it was decided that women might hold the imperial government.

4. Tlas reigned 17 years.

5. Sĕthĕnēs reigned 41 years.

6. Chæres (*reigned*) 17 years.

7. Nĕphĕrchĕrēs (reigned) 25 years. In his time it is said that the Nile flowed with honey during eleven days.

8. Sesōchris, whose height was five cubits and his breadth three, (reigned) 48 years.

9. Chenerēs 30 years.

The whole number of years is 302.


## THE THIRD DYNASTY,

Of nine Memphite kings.

1. Necherōphēs reigned 28 years. In his time the Libyans revolted from the Egyptians ; but, on account of an unexpected increase of the moon, they surrendered themselves for fear.

2. Tosorthrus reigned 29 years. He is called Asclepius [*i.e.*, Aesculapius], by the Egyptians, for his medical knowledge. He built a house of hewn stones, and greatly patronised writing.

3. Tyris reigned 7 years.

4. Mesōchris 17 years.
5. Soïphis [*or*, Sōŭphis] 16 years.
6. Tosĕrtasis 19 years.
7. Achis [*or*, Achēs] 42 years.
8. Siphuris 30 years.
9. Kĕrphĕrēs 26 years.
Altogether 214 years.

### THE FOURTH DYNASTY,

Of eight Memphite kings of a different race.
1. Sōris reigned 29 years.
2. Suphis reigned 63 years. He built the largest pyramid. He was also called Peroptes, and was translated to the gods, and wrote the sacred book.
3. Suphis (or Cheops) reigned 66 years.
4. Mencherēs (Men-ke-ra) 63 years.
5. Ratoeses 25 years.
6. Bicheres 22 years.
7. Sĕbĕrchĕrēs 7 years.
8. Thamphthis 9 years.
Altogether 274 years [*or* 284, according to the correct computation.]

### THE FIFTH DYNASTY,

Consisting of nine Elephantine kings.
1. Usercheris reigned 28 years.
2. Sephrēs 13 years.
3. Nephercherēs 20 years.

4. Sisiris 7 years.
5. Cherēs 20 years.
6. Rathuris 44 years.
7. Mencherēs 9 years.
8. Tarcherēs [*or*, Tatcherēs] 44 years.
9. Obnos [*or*, Onnos] 33 years.
Altogether 248 years [*or*, 2ı8 years.]

## THE SIXTH DYNASTY,

Consisting of six Memphite kings.
1. Othŏēs, 30 years, who was killed by his guards.
2. Phius reigned 53 years.
3. Methūsūphis 7 years.
4. Phiŏps, who began to reign at six years of age, and reigned till he had completed his hundredth year.
5. Menthesuphis reigned one year.
6. Nitōcris, who was the most handsome woman of her time, of a fair complexion; she built the third pyramid, and reigned ı2 years.
Altogether 203 years.

## THE SEVENTH DYNASTY,

Of seventy Memphite kings, who reigned 70 days.

## THE EIGHTH DYNASTY,

Of twenty-seven Memphite kings, who reigned ı46 years.

### THE NINTH DYNASTY,

Of nineteen Heracleotic kings, who reigned 409 years.

1. The first was Achthoës, the worst of all his predecessors. He did much harm to all the inhabitants of Egypt, was seized with madness, and killed by a crocodile.

### THE TENTH DYNASTY,

Consisting of nineteen Heracleotic kings, who reigned 185 years.

### THE ELEVENTH DYNASTY,

Consisting of sixteen Diospolite, (or Theban), kings, who reigned 43 years.

Among them Ammenemes, who reigned 16 years.

The sum total of the above-named kings is 192, who reigned 2,308 years and 70 days.—*From Syncellus Chronicon, 54 to 59—Euseb. Chron.,* 14 *and* 15.

# THE SECOND BOOK OF MANĚTHO.

## THE TWELFTH DYNASTY,

OF seven Diospolite, (or Theban), kings.

1. Geson Goses [*or*, Sesonchōsis; *or*, Sesortŏsis; *or*, Sesortōsis], the son of Ammanemes. He reigned 46 years.

2. Ammanemēs reigned 38 years. He was slain by his eunuchs.

3. Sesostris 41 [*or*, 48] years. He conquered all Asia in nine years, and Europe as far as Thrace; everywhere erecting monuments of his conquests of those nations; statues of men among nations who acted bravely, but among the degenerate he erected figures of women, engraving their sexual organs upon the pillars. By the Egyptians he is supposed to be the first after Osiris.

4. Lacharēs 8 years, who built the Labyrinth in Arsenoïte [*sic*] as a tomb for himself.

5. Ammerēs reigned 8 years.

6. Ammenemēs 8 years.

7. Skĕmiŏphris, his sister, 4 years.

Altogether 160 years.

## THE THIRTEENTH DYNASTY

Consisted of 60 Diospolite, (or Theban), kings, whose names are lost. They reigned 453 years (*according to the Armenian copy of Eusebius*).

### THE FOURTEENTH DYNASTY.

Consisting of 76 Xoite kings, who ruled 184 [or, 484] years. (The number 484 is from the Armenian version of Eusebius.)

The names are entirely lost.

### THE FIFTEENTH[1] DYNASTY

Of the Hyk-shos or Shepherd-Kings.

There were six foreign, *i.e.*, Phœnician or Canaanitish kings. This dynasty took Memphis, and built a city in the Sethroïte nome, whence they made an invasion, and conquered all Egypt. Of these—

1. Saïtēs [or, Salatis] reigned 19 years, after whom the Saite nome or district is called.
2. Beon [or, Bnōn] reigned 44 years.
3. Pachnan [or, Apachnas] 61 years.
4. Staan 50 years.
5. Archlës [or, Assis] 49 years.
6. Aphōbis [or, Apōphis] 61 years.

Altogether 284 years.

### THE SIXTEENTH DYNASTY

Of 32 Grecian shepherds, who reigned 518 years.

### THE SEVENTEENTH DYNASTY

Consisted of 43 shepherd-kings and 43 Thebans, [or, Diospolites.]

---

[1] This is the Seventeenth Dynasty according to Eusebius.

The Shepherds and Thebans reigned altogether 151 years.

## THE EIGHTEENTH DYNASTY,

Of sixteen Diospolite, (*or*, Theban), kings.

1. Amōs ; in whose time Moses went forth from Egypt, as we have shown.
2. Chebrōs 13 years.
3. Amenōphthis 24 years.
4. Amersis [*or*, Amensis] 22 years.
5. Misaphris 13 years.
6. Misphragmuthōsis 26 years, in whose time the Flood of Deucalion happened.
7. Tuthmōsis reigned 9 years.
8. Amenōphis 31 years.   He is supposed to be the Memnon, to whom the musical statue[1] (in Egypt) was erected.
9. Hōrus reigned 37 years.
10. Acherrhes [*or*, Akenchres] 32 years.
11. Rathōs [*or*, Rathōtis] 6 years.
12. Chebrēs 12 years.
13. Acherrhēs [*or*, Akenchrēs] 12 years.
14. Armessēs [*or*, Armais] 5 years.
15. Ramĕssēs 1 year.
16. Amenōph [*or*, Amenōphath] 19 years.
Altogether 263 [*or*, 259].

---

[1] The researches of Pococke and Hamilton have long since proved this to be the Memnon of the Ancients, while the hieroglyphic labours of Champollion have established the claims of Amenoph to the statues he erected.

### THE NINETEENTH DYNASTY,

Consisted of seven Diospolite, (or Theban), kings.

1. Sĕthōs reigned 51 years.
2. Rapsakes [or, Rampsēs] 61 years.
3. Ammenĕphthēs 20 years.
4. Ramĕsēs 60 years.
5. Ammenemnēs [or, Ammĕnĕmēs] 5 years.
6. Thuōris, who is called by Homer, Polybus.
7. Alcandrus, 7 years, in whose time Ilion, (*i.e.*, Troy), was taken.

Altogether 209 years.

In this second book of Manĕtho are contained 96 kings, and 2121 years.—*Syncel. Chron.* 59 *to* 75. —*Euseb. Chron.* 15 *to* 17.

# THE THIRD BOOK OF MANĔTHO.

## THE TWENTIETH DYNASTY,

Of 12 Diospolite, (or Theban), kings, who reigned 135 years.

## THE TWENTY-FIRST DYNASTY,

Of seven Tanite kings.

1. Smĕdēs [or, Smĕndēs] reigned 26 years.
2. Psusĕnēs, or Psunĕsēs, 46 years.
3. Nephĕrchĕrēs 4 years.
4. Amenōphthis 9 years.
5. Osochōr 6 years.
6. Psinaches 9 years.
7. Susenes [or, Psusĕnnēs] 30 years.

Altogether 130 years.

## THE TWENTY-SECOND DYNASTY,

Of nine Bubastite kings.

1. Sesonchis (or Shishak)[1] 21 years.
2. Osoroth [or, Osōrthōn] 15 years.
3, 4, 5. Three others reigned 25 years.

---

[1] See 1 Kings xi. 40.

6. Takellôthis[1] 13 years.
7, 8, 9. Three others 42 years.
Altogether reigned 120 years.

## THE TWENTY-THIRD DYNASTY,

Of four Tanite kings.
1. Petoubatēs reigned 40 years, in whose time the
Olympiads began.
2. Osŏrchō 8 years, whom the Egyptians call
Hercules.
3. Psammus 10 years.
4. Zeet 31 years.
Altogether 89 years.

## THE TWENTY-FOURTH DYNASTY.

Bocchoris, [*or* Bonchôris], the Saite, reigned 6
years, in whose reign (a miracle occurred), for a
sheep spoke.
Total 990 years.

## THE TWENTY-FIFTH DYNASTY,

Consisted of 3 Ethiopic kings.
1. Sabbakōn, who having taken Bocchoris captive,
burnt him alive, and reigned 8 years.

---

[1] Perhaps Tiglath Pileser, king of Assyria, or some one
ruling as a tributary to the Assyrian monarch.

2. Sevechus,[1] his son, who reigned 14 years.

3. Tarkos, or Tarakos [Tirhakah],[2] 18 years.
Altogether 40 years.

## THE TWENTY-SIXTH DYNASTY,

Consisting of 9 Saite kings.

1. Stephinates reigned 7 years.

2. Nechepsōs reigned 6 years.

3. Nechao (or Necho) 8 years.

4. Psammitichus 54 years.

5. Nechao, (or Necho), the 2nd reigned 6 years.
He took Jerusalem, and carried away captive Joahaz,
the king, to Egypt.

6. Psammuthis 6 years.

7. Vaphris (or Hophra) 19 years, to whom the
remainder of the Jews fled when Jerusalem was
taken by the Assyrians.

8. Amōsis 44 years.

9. Psammacherites[3] 6 months.
Altogether 150 years and six months.

## THE TWENTY-SEVENTH DYNASTY,

Of eight Persian kings.

1. Cambyses reigned over Persia, his own king·
dom, 5 years, and over Egypt 6 years.

---

[1] Called So, or Sevé, in 2 Kings xvii. 4.

[2] 2 Kings xix. 9.

[3] Eusebius omits the last king, and inserts Ammĕrēs at
the beginning as the first.

2. Darius, the son of Hystaspes, 36 years.
3. Xerxes the Great 21 years.
4. Artabanus 7 months.[1]
5. Artaxerxes 41 years.
6. Xerxes 2 months.
7. Sogdianus 7 months.
8. Darius, the son of Xerxes, 19 years.
Altogether 124 years and four months.

### THE TWENTY-EIGHTH DYNASTY.

Amyrteos, the Saite, reigned 6 years.

### THE TWENTY-NINTH DYNASTY,

Consisting of four Mendesian kings.
1. Nepherites reigned 6 years.
2. Achōris 13 years.
3. Psammūthis 1 year.
4. Nephorites 4 months.
5. Muthis 1 year.
Altogether 20 years and four months.

### THE THIRTIETH DYNASTY,

Consisting of three Sebennyte kings.
1. Nĕctanĕbēs reigned 18 years.

---

[1] Eusebius omits Artabanus, and between Cambyses and Darius places the Magi, with a reign of seven months.

2. Teōs 2 years.

3. Nectanĕbos 18 years.

Altogether 38 years.

## THE THIRTY-FIRST DYNASTY,

Consisting of three Persian kings.

1. (Darius) Ochus, who ruled Persia 20 years and Egypt two years.

2. Arses, or Arses Ochus, (or Artaxerxes), reigned 3 years.

3. Darius 4 years.

Altogether 9 years.

Total 1,050 years.

*From Syncell. Chron. 73 to 78 and Euseb. Chron. 16, 17.*

*Note by the Editor.* For the different readings of the royal names, the length of their respective reigns, and the sum total of the years, which are often divergent, I must refer the student to Vol. i. of Dr. Birch's edition of Bunsen's *Egypt's Place in History*, Appendix, p. 642—736, where, in Greek and Latin, will be found the lists of Syncellus, Eusebius, Eratosthenes, and others.

# MANÉTHO.

---

## OF THE SHEPHERD-KINGS.

"WE had formerly a king whose name was Timaus. In his time it came to pass, I know not how, that God was displeased with us : and there came up from the East, in a strange manner, men of an ignoble race, who had the confidence to invade our country, and easily subdued it by their power, without a battle. And, when they had our rulers in their hands, they burnt our cities, and demolished the temples of the gods, and inflicted every kind of barbarity upon the inhabitants, slaying some, and reducing the wives and children of others to a state of slavery. At length they made one of themselves king, whose name was Salatis : he lived at Memphis, and rendered both the upper and lower regions of Egypt tributary, and stationed garrisons in places which were best adapted for that purpose. But he directed his attention principally to the security of the eastern frontier ; for he regarded with suspicion the increasing power of the Assyrians, who, he foresaw, would one day undertake an invasion of the kingdom. And, observing in the Saïte nome, upon the east of the Bubastite channel, a city which from some ancient theological reference was called Avaris ;

and finding it admirably adapted to his purpose, he
rebuilt it, and strongly fortified it with walls, and
garrisoned it with a force of two hundred and fifty
thousand armed men.    To this city Salatis repaired
in summer time, to collect his tribute, and pay his
troops, and to exercise his soldiers, in order to strike
terror into foreigners.

And Salatis died after a reign of nineteen years ;
after him reigned Beon forty-four years ; and he was
succeeded by Apachnas, who reigned thirty-six years
and seven months; after him reigned Apophis sixty-
one years, and Ianias fifty years and one month.
After all these reigned Assis forty-nine years and
two months. These six were the first rulers amongst
them, and, during all the period of their dynasty,
they made war upon the Egyptians, in hope of
exterminating the whole race.    All this nation was
styled Hyk-shos, that is, the Shepherd-Kings ; for
the first syllable, Hyk, according to the sacred
dialect, denotes *king*, and *sos* signifies a shepherd ;
but this according to the vulgar tongue ; and, of
these two words is compounded the term *Hyk-shos*,
whom some say were Arabians.    This people, thus
denominated Shepherd-Kings, and their descendants
retained possession of Egypt for the space of 511
years.

After these things, he (Manĕtho), relates that the
kings of Thebaïs, and of the other parts of Egypt,
made an insurrection against the Shepherds ; · and,

that a long and mighty war was carried on between
them, till the Shepherds were subdued by a king
whose name was Alisphragmuthōsis ; and, that they
were by him driven out of the rest of Egypt, and
shut up within a space containing ten thousand acres,
which was called Avaris.   All this tract of country,
(says Manĕtho), the Shepherds surrounded with a
vast and strong wall, that they might retain all their
possessions and their booty within a fortress.

And Thummōsis, the son of Alisphragmuthōsis,
endeavoured to force them by a siege, and beleaguered
the place with a body of four hundred and eighty
thousand men ; but, at the moment when he despaired
of reducing them by siege, they agreed to a capitulation, that they would leave Egypt, and should be
permitted to go out, without molestation, whereso-
ever they pleased.   And, according to this stipulation,
they departed from Egypt with all their families and
effects, in number not less than two hundred and
forty thousand, and bent their way through the
desert towards Syria.   But, as they stood in fear of
the Assyrians, who had then dominion over Asia,
they built a city, in that country which is now called
Judæa, of sufficient size to contain this multitude of
men, and named it Jerusalem.

(In another book of the Egyptian histories,
Manĕtho says), That this people, who are here called
Shepherds, in their sacred books were also styled
Captives.

After the departure of this nation of Shepherds to Jerusalem, Tethmōsis, the king of Egypt, who drove them out, reigned twenty-five years and four months, and then died ; after him his son, Chebron, took the government into his hands for thirteen years ; after him reigned Amenōphis for twenty years and seven months ; then his sister Amessēs, 21 years and nine months.

She was succeeded by Mephrēs, who reigned 12 years and nine months ; after him Mephramuthōsis, who reigned 25 years and 10 months ; then Thmōsis, who reigned nine years and eight months ; after whom Amenōphis reigned 30 years and 10 months ; then Orus (Horus), who reigned 36 and five months ; then his daughter Akenchrēs, who reigned 12 years and one month ; and after her, Rathōtis for nine years ; then Akencheres 12 years and five months, and another Akencheres 12 years and three months ; after him, Armaïs reigned four years and one month ; and Ramĕssēs (the Great) one year and four months ; then Armesses, (*i.e.*, Ramses), the son of Miammoun, who reigned 66 years and two months ; after him Amenophis for 19 years and six months ; he was succeeded by Sethosis, who is called Ramesses, who maintained an army of cavalry and a naval force.

This king, (Sethosis), appointed his brother Armaïs as his viceroy over Egypt. He also invested him with all the other authority of a king, but with the following restrictions, viz.—1st, That he should not

I

wear the crown ; 2nd, Nor interfere with the queen, the mother of his children ; 3rd, Nor abuse the royal concubines. Sethosis then made an expedition against the island of Cyprus, and Phœnicia, and waged war with the Assyrians and Medes ; and he subdued them all, some by force of arms, and others without a blow, by the mere terror of his power. And being puffed up with his success, he advanced still more confidently, and overthrew the cities, and subdued the countries of the East.

But Armaïs, who was left in Egypt, took advantage of the opportunity, and fearlessly committed all those acts which his brother had enjoined him not to do ; he violated the queen, and continued an unrestrained intercourse with the concubines, and, at the persuasion of his friends, he assumed the diadem, and openly opposed his brother.

But the ruler over the priests of Egypt sent to Sethosis, and informed him of what had happened, and how his brother had set himself up in opposition to his power. Upon this Sethosis immediately returned to Pelusium, and recovered his kingdom. The country of Egypt took its name from Sethosis, who was called also Ægyptus, as was his brother Armaïs known by the name of Danaus." [1]—*Joseph. contr. Ap.* lib. I. c. 14, 15.

---

[1] Danaus was the first king of the Argives.

## OF THE ISRAELITES.

" This king, (Amenophis), was desirous of behold-
ing the gods, since Horus, one of his predecessors in
the kingdom had seen them. He communicated his
desire to a priest of the same name with himself,
Amenophis, the son of Papis ; one who seemed to
partake of the divine nature, both in his wisdom and
in his knowledge of futurity.

Amenophis returned him for answer, that he
might behold the gods if he would cleanse the land
of all lepers, and other unclean persons that were in
it. Well pleased with this information, the king
gathered together out of the land of Egypt all that
laboured under any defect of body, to the number of
80,000, and sent them to the quarries, (*in the Mafra,
or, Sinaitic peninsula*), which are situated on the east
side of the Nile, that they might work in them, and
be separated from the rest of the Egyptians.

And he, (Manĕtho), says, there were among them
some learned priests who were (also) infected with
the leprosy. And Amenophis, the wise man and
prophet, fearing lest the vengeance of the gods
should fall, both on himself and on the king, should
it appear that violence had been used towards them,
added this also in a prophetic spirit ;—that certain
people would come to the assistance of these polluted wretches, and would subdue Egypt, and hold
it in possession for thirteen years. These tidings

however he dared not to communicate to the king, but left in writing an account of what should come to pass, and destroyed himself; at which the king was fearfully distressed.

' (After which, he writes thus, word for word): When those that were sent to work in the quarries had continued for some time in that miserable state, the king was petitioned to set apart for their habitation and protection the city Avaris, which had been left desolate by the Shepherds; and he granted them their desire: now this city, according to the ancient theology, is a Typhonian[1] city.

When these men had taken possession of the city, and found it well adapted for a revolt, they appointed over themselves a ruler out of the priests of Heliopolis,[2] one whose name was Osarsiph,[3] and they bound 'themselves by oath that they would be obedient. Osarsiph then, in the first place enacted this law, that they should neither worship the [*Egyptian*] gods, nor abstain from (*eating*) any of those sacred animals which the Egyptians hold in the highest veneration, but sacrifice and slay them all; and that

---

[1] TYPHON was the Ahriman, or Satan, of the Egyptian theology. " Down to the time of Rameses, B.C. 1300, he was one of the most venerated and powerful gods. After about 970 B.C. he was regarded as the foe of Osiris and all the gods of Egypt."—BUNSEN'S *Egypt's Place*, vol. i., p. 456.

[2] Called ON in Genesis xli. 45, 50; AN in Egyptian.

[3] By Osarsiph he means Moses, the Jewish lawgiver and deliverer.

they should connect themselves with none but such as were of that confederacy. When he had made such laws as these, and many others of a tendency directly in opposition to the customs of the Egyptians, he gave orders that they should employ the multitude of hands in rebuilding the walls about the city (Avaris), and hold themselves in readiness for war with Amenophis the king; whilst he (Osarsiph) took into his confidence and counsels some others of the priests and unclean persons. He then sent ambassadors to the city called Jerusalem; to those Shepherds who had been expelled by Tethmosis,[1] whereby he informed them of the affairs of himself, and of the others who had been treated in the same ignominious manner, and requested they would come with one consent, to his assistance in this war against Egypt. He also promised in the first place to reinstate them in their ancient city and country, Avaris, and provide a plentiful maintenance for their numerous host, and fight for them as occasion might require. He informed them, moreover, that they could easily reduce the land (of Egypt) under their dominion. The Shepherds received this message with the greatest joy, and quickly mustered to the number of 200,000 men, and came up to Avaris. Now Amenophis, king of Egypt, when he was informed of their invasion, was in great consternation, remembering the prophecy of Amenophis,

---

[1] Tethmosis was a sovereign of the 18th dynasty, according to Eusebius.

the son of Papis, and he assembled the armies of
the Egyptians, and took counsel with the leaders,
and commanded the sacred animals to be brought to
him, especially those which were held in the greatest
veneration in the temples, and particularly charged
the priests to conceal the images of their gods with
the utmost care.   And his son Sethos, who was also
called Ramesses from his father Rampses, being but
five years old he committed to the protection of a
friend.   And he marched with the rest of the Egyptians, being three hundred thousand warriors, against
the enemy, who advanced to meet him; but he did
not attack them, thinking it would be to wage war
against the gods, but he returned, and came again to
Memphis, where he took Apis, (*the sacred bull*), and
the other sacred animals he had sent for, and retreated
immediately into Ethiopia, together with all his army,
and all the multitude of the Egyptians: for the king
of Ethiopia was under obligations to him, wherefore
he received him kindly, and took care of all the multitude that was with him, while the country supplied
all that was necessary for their food.   He also allotted
to him cities and villages during his exile, which was
to continue from its beginning during the predestined
thirteen years.   Moreover, he pitched a camp for an
Ethiopian army upon the borders of Egypt, as a
protection to king Amenophis.

While such was the state of things in Ethiopia,
the people of Jerusalem, having come down in company with the unclean of the Egyptians, treated the

inhabitants with such barbarity that those who wit-
nessed their impieties believed that their joint sway
was more execrable than that which the Shepherds
(*alone*) had formerly exercised. They not only set
fire to the cities and villages, but committed every
kind of sacrilege, and destroyed the images of the
gods, and roasted and fed upon those sacred animals
that were worshipped; and having compelled the
priests and prophets to kill and sacrifice them, they
cast them naked out of the country.

It is also said that the priest who ordained their
polity and laws was by birth a native of Heliopolis,
and that he was named Osarsiph, from Osiris, the
god venerated at Heliopolis. He adds, however,
that when he went over to these people his name
was changed, and he was called Moÿses (Moüses or
Moses). Manĕtho again says, 'after this Amenophis
returned from Ethiopia with a great force, and
Rampses his son also, with other forces, and encoun-
tering the Shepherds and the unclean people, they
defeated them, and slew multitudes of them, and pursued the remainder to the borders of Syria (Judea).'"
—*From Josephus against Apion.* Book i., cap. 27.

---

"The authenticity of the account of Josephus," says Dr.
Eisenlohr, "is not to be doubted, for, if he had not found
the story in Manetho, he would not have thought it necessary to denounce it. It has long been accepted by Egyptologists," says he, "that the narration of Josephus refers
really to the Exodus of the Israelites."—*Transactions of
Soc. Bib. Archæol.* vol. i., part 2., p. 380—1.—*Note by the
Editor.*

"Among the Egyptians there is a certain tablet called the Old Chronicle, containing thirty dynasties in 113 descents, during the long period of 36,525 years. The first series of princes was that of the Auritæ; the second was that of the Mestræans; the third of Egyptians. The Chronicle runs as follows :—

To Hephæstus [or, Vulcan] is assigned no time, as he is apparent both by night and day.

Helius [or, the Sun] the son of Hephæstus (Vulcan) reigned three myriads of years.

Then Kronus [or, Saturn] and the other twelve divinities reigned 3,984 years.

Next in order are the demigods, in number eight, who reigned 217 years.

After these are enumerated 15 generations of the Cynic circle, which take up 443 years.

The 16th Dynasty is of the Tanites, eight kings, which lasted 190 years.

17th, Memphites; 4 in descent; 103 years.

18th, Memphites; 14 in descent; 348 years.

19th, Diospolites (or Thebans); 5 in descent; 194 years.

20th, Diospolites (or Thebans); 8 in descent; 228 years.

21st, Tanites; 6 in descent; 121 years.

22nd, Tanites ; 3 in descent ; 48 years.

23rd, Diospolites (or Thebans) ; 2 in descent ; 19 years.

24th, Saïtes ; 3 in descent ; 44 years.

25th, Ethiopians ; 3 in descent ; 44 years.

26th, Memphites ; 7 in descent ; 177 years.

27th, Persians ; 5 in descent ; 124 years.

28th (No information).

29th, Tanites ;   in descent ; 39 years.

30th, A Tanite ; 1 in descent ; 18 years.

Embracing in all 30 Dynasties, and amounting to 36,525 years."—*From Syncellus' Chronicon*. 51, *and Eusebius' Chron*. 6.

## Canon of the Kings of Thebes.

---

The first who reigned was Mines, (Menes), the Thebinite, the Thebæan ; which is by interpretation Dionius.[1]  He reigned sixty-two years, and lived in the year of the world 2,900.

The 2nd of the Theban kings reigned Athothes the son of Mines (Menes), 59 years.  He is called by interpretation Hermogenes.  In the year of the world 2,962.

The 3rd of the Theban Egyptian kings was Athothes, of the same name, 32 years.  In the year of the world 3,021.

The 4th of the Theban kings was Diabies, the son of Athothes, 19 years.  By interpretation he is called Philesteros.  In the year of the world 3,053.

The 5th of the Theban kings was Pemphos, the son of Athothes, who is called Heraclides.  He reigned 18 years.  In the year of the world 3,072.

The 6th of the Theban Egyptian kings was Tœgar Amachus Momchiri, the Memphite, who is called a

---

[1] *i.c.*, a Diospolitan ; for Thebes, (called No in our Bibles), was designated by the Greeks as *Diospolis ; i.c.* the city of Jupiter (Ammon.)

man redundant in his members, 79 years and A.M. 3,090.

The 7th of the Theban Egyptian kings, Stœchus his son, who is Ares the senseless, reigned 6 years, A.M. 3,169.

The 8th of the Theban Egyptian kings Gosormies, who is called Etesipantus, reigned 30 years, and A.M. 3,175.

The 9th of the Theban Egyptian kings Mares, his son, who is called Heliodorus, 26 years, and A.M. 3,205.

The 10th of the Theban Egyptian kings Anoÿphes, which signifies a common son, reigned 20 years, and A.M. 3,231.

The 11th of the Theban Egyptian kings Sirius, which signifies the son of the cheek, but, according to others Abascantus, reigned 18 years, and A.M. 3,251.

The 12th of the Theban Egyptian kings reigned Chnubus Gneurus, which is Chryses the son of Chryses, 22 years, A.M. 3,269.

The 13th of the Theban Egyptian kings reigned Ranosis, which is Archicrator, 13 years, A.M. 3,291.

The 14th of the Theban Egyptian kings, Biuris, reigned 10 years. Anno Mundi 3,304.

The 15th of the Theban kings, Saophis Komastes, or according to some, Chrematistes (*i.e.*, the trafficker, or money-getter), reigned 29 years, and this was about A.M. 3,314.

The 16th of the Theban kings, Sensaophis the 2nd, reigned 27 years, A.M. 3,343.

The 17th of the Theban kings, Moscheris Heliodotus, reigned 31 years, A.M. 3,370.

The 18th of the Theban kings, Musthis, reigned 33 years, A.M. 3,401.

The 19th of the Theban kings, Pammus Archondes, reigned 35 years, A.M. 3,434.

The 20th of the Theban kings, Apaphus, surnamed the Great, is said to have reigned 100 years, with the exception of one hour, A.M. 3,469.

The 21st of the Theban kings, Acheskus Okaras, reigned one year, A.M. 3,569.

The 22nd of the Theban sovereigns was Nitokris, who reigned instead of her husband (she is Athena Nikephorus.   Her reign was 6 years, A.M. 3,570.)

The 23rd of the Theban kings, Myrtaeus Ammonodotus, reigned 22 years, A.M. 3,576.

The 24th of the Theban kings, Thyosimares the Robust, who is called the sun, reigned 12 years, A.M. 3598.

The 25th of the Theban kings, Thinillus, which is the augmenter of the country's strength, reigned 8 years, A.M. 3,610.

The 26th of the Theban kings, Semphrucrates, who is Hercules Harpocrates, reigned 18 years, A.M. 3,618.

The 27th of the Theban kings, Chuthur Taurus the tyrant, 7 years, A.M. 3,636.

The 28th of the Theban kings, Meures Philoscorus, reigned 12 years, A.M. 3,643.

The 29th of the Theban kings, Chomaephtha, Cosmus Philephæstus, reigned 11 years, A.M. 3,655.

The 30th of the Theban kings, Ancunius Ochytyrannus, reigned 60 years, A.M. 3,666.

The 31st of the Theban kings, Penteathyris, reigned 42 years, A.M. 3,726.

The 32nd of the Theban kings, Stamenemes the second, reigned 23 years, A.M. 3,768.

The 33rd of the Theban kings, Sistosichermes, the strength of Hercules, reigned 55 years, A.M. 3,791.

The 34th of the Theban kings, Maris, reigned 43 years, A.M. 3,846.

The 35th of the Theban kings, Siphoas, who is Hermes (Mercury), the son of Hephaestus, reigned 5 years, A.M. 3,889.

The 36th of the Theban kings, . . . . , reigned 14 years, A.M. 3,894.

The 37th of the Theban kings, Phruron, who is Nilus, reigned 5 years, A.M. 3,908.

The 38th of the Theban kings, Amuthantaeus, reigned 63 years, A.M. 3,913.

*From Syncellus's Chronicon,* 91, 96, 101, 104, 109, 123, 147.

## OF THE EXODUS.

### FROM CHAEREMON.

"AFTER him, (*i.e.*, Manetho), I wish to examine Chaeremon, who professes to have composed a history of Egypt. He gives the same name as does Manětho to the king Amenōphis, and his son Ramesses, and says as follows :—

Isis appeared to Amenophis in his dreams, rebuking him that her temple should have been overthrown in war. Upon which Phritiphantes, the sacred scribe, told him that if he would clear Egypt of all polluted persons, he would be delivered from these terrors. He therefore collected 250,000 unclean persons, and drove them out (of Egypt). Their leaders were two scribes, called Moÿses and Josephus ; the latter of whom was a sacred scribe : but their Egyptian names were respectively, that of Moÿses *Tisithēne*, and that of Josephus *Peteseph*. They bent their way towards Pelusium, where they met with 380,000 men left there by Amenophis, whom he would not suffer to come into Egypt. With these they made a treaty, and invaded Egypt. But Amenophis waited not to oppose their incursion, but fled into Ethiopia, leaving his wife pregnant : and she concealed herself in a cavern, where she brought forth a child, and named him Messenes, who, when he arrived at manhood, drove out the Jews into Syria, being about 200,000, and recalled his father, Amenophis, from Ethiopia."—*Extracted from Josephus against Apion*, Book i. ch. 32.

## From Diodorus Siculus.

" There having arisen in former days a pestiferous disease in Egypt, the multitude attributed the cause of the evil to the Deity ; for a very great concourse of foreigners of every nation then dwelt in Egypt, who were addicted to strange rites in their worship and sacrifices ; so that, in consequence, the due honours of the gods fell into disuse. Whence the native inhabitants of the land inferred, that unless they removed them, there would never be an end of their distresses. They immediately, therefore, expelled these foreigners ; the most illustrious and able of whom passed over in a body, (as some say), into Greece, and other places, under the conduct of celebrated leaders, of whom the most renowned were Danaus, and Cadmus. But a large body of the people went forth into the country which is now called Judea, situated not far distant from Egypt, being altogether desert in those times. The leader of this colony was Moses, a man very remarkable for his great wisdom and valour. When he had taken possession of the land, among other cities, he founded that which is called Jerusalem, which is now the most celebrated."—*Extracted from Book* xl. *Ecl.* 1, p. 921.

*Note.— The rest of the fragment gives an account of the Jewish polity, laws, &c. It was the beginning of Diodorus's "History of the Jewish War," and is preserved by Photius, (Bishop of Constantinople.)*

### From Lysimachus.

" He says, that in the reign of Bocchŏris, king of Egypt, the Jewish people, being infected with leprosy, scurvy, and sundry other diseases, took shelter in the temples, where they begged for food ; and that, in consequence of the vast number of persons who were seized with these complaints, there arose a famine in Egypt. Upon this, Bocchŏris, king of the Egyptians, sent persons to enquire of the Oracle of Ammon,[1] respecting this scarcity, and the god directed him to cleanse the temples of all polluted and impious men, and to cast them out into the desert, but to drown those who were affected with the leprosy and scurvy, inasmuch as their existence was displeasing to the Sun; then to purify the temples, upon which the land would recover its fertility. When Bocchŏris had received the oracle, he as-

---

[1] The temple of Jupiter Ammon was situated in the Oasis of Siwah, as it is now called.

sembled the priests and attendants of the altars, and commanded them to gather together all the unclean persons and deliver them over to the soldiers to lead them forth into the desert ; but to wrap the lepers in sheets of lead, and cast them into the sea. After they had drowned those afflicted with the leprosy and scurvy, they collected the rest, and left them to perish in the desert. But they took counsel among themselves, and when night came on they lighted up fires and torches to defend themselves, and fasted all the next night to propitiate the gods to save them. Upon the following day a certain man, called Moÿses, counselled them to persevere in following one direct way till they should arrive at habitable places, and enjoined them to hold no friendly communication with men, neither to follow those things which men esteemed good, but such as were considered evil ; and to overthrow the temples and altars of the gods as often as they should meet with them. When they had assented to these.proposals, they continued their journey through the desert, acting upon those rules, and after severe hardships, they at length arrived in a habitable country, where, having inflicted every kind of injury upon the inhabitants, plundering and burning the temples, they came at length to the land which is now called Judea, and founded a city and settled there. This city was named Hierosyla,[1]

---

[1] From ἱερος, a temple, and συλαω, to plunder.

from their (*plundering and sacrilegious*) disposition.
But in after times, when they acquired strength
to obliterate the reproach, they changed its name,
and called the city Hierosolyma, and themselves
Hierosolymites."—*Extracted from Josephus against
Apion*, 34.


## FROM POLEMO.

"Some of the Greeks also relate that Moses
flourished in those times.    Polemo, in the first book
of his Grecian histories, says 'that in the reign of
Apis, the son of Phoroneus, a part of the Egyptian
army deserted from Egypt, and took up their
habitation in that part of Syria which is called
Palestine, not far from Arabia.'   These indeed were
they who went out with Moses."—*Extracted from
Africanus, as quoted by Eusebius, Præp. Evang.*,
Book x.


## FROM PTOLEMAEUS MENDESIUS.

"Amosis, who lived about the same time with
Inachus the Argive (*i.e.*, the king of Argos), overthrew the city of Avaris, as Ptolemæus Mendesius
has related in his chronicle."—*Extracted from the
Stromata of Clemens, Bishop of Alexandria, quoted
by Eusebius, Præp. Evang.*, Book x.

## FROM ARTABANUS.

"And they (*the Jews*) borrowed of the Egyptians many vessels, and no small quantity of raiment, and every variety of treasure, and passed over the branches of the river towards Arabia, and upon the third day's march they arrived at a convenient station upon the Red Sea. And the Memphites say that Moÿses, being well acquainted with that part of the country, waited for the ebbing tide, and then made the whole multitude pass through the shallows of the sea. But the Heliopolitans (or people of On), say that the king pursued them with a great army, and took with him the sacred animals, in order to recover the substance which the Jews had borrowed of the Egyptians. But that a divine voice instructed Moÿses to strike the sea with his rod : and that when Moÿses heard this, he touched the waters with his rod, whereupon the waves stood apart, and the host went through along a dry path. He says, moreover, that when the Egyptians came up with them, and pursued them, the fire flashed on them from before, and the sea again inundated the path, and that all the Egyptians perished either by the fire or by the return of the waters.

But the Jews escaped the danger, and passed thirty years in the desert, where God rained upon them a kind of grain called panic,[1] whose colour was like

---

[1] ἐλυμος.

snow. He says also that Moÿses was ruddy, with white hair, and of a dignified deportment, and that when he did these things, he was in the eighty-ninth year of his age."—*Extracted from Eusebius, Praep. Evang.*, Book x.

*Artabanus, evidently an Alexandrian Jew, is said to have written about a century before Christ. The fragments of his history which have been preserved follow the Scriptures, with some few variations and additions. In this account both the Memphite and the Heliopolitan traditions are referred to. Unfortunately its authenticity is very much to be suspected.*

---

## THE OBELISK OF HELIOPOLIS.

### From Ammianus Marcellinus.

The interpretation begins upon the southern side.

### South Side.

*Verse the First.*

" The Sun to king Rhamestes. I have bestowed upon you to rule graciously over all the world. He whom the Sun loves is Horus the Brave, the lover of truth, the son of Heron, born of God, the Restorer of the World : He whom the sun has chosen is the king Rhamestes, valiant in battle, to whom all the earth is subject by his might and bravery. Rhamestes the king, the immortal offspring of the Sun."

### Verse the Second.

"It is Horus the Brave who is in truth appointed the Lord of the Diadem; he who renders Egypt glorious and possesses it; he who sheds a splendour over Heliopolis, and Regenerates the rest of the world, and Honours the gods who dwell in Heliopolis, him the Sun loves.

### Verse the Third.

Horus the Brave, the offspring of the Sun, All-glorious: whom the Sun has chosen, and the valiant Ares (Mars) has endowed. His goodness remains for ever, whom Ammon loves, who fills with good the temple of the Phœnix. To him the Gods have granted life, Horus the brave, the son of Heron Rhamestes, the king of the world: He has protected Egypt and subdued her neighbours: Him the Sun loves. The gods have granted him great length of life. He is Rhamestes, the Lord of the World, the Immortal.

### ANOTHER SIDE.

### Verse the Second.

"I the Sun, the great God, the sovereign of heaven, have bestowed upon you life without satiety.

Horus the Brave, Lord of the diadem, incomparable, the Sovereign of Egypt, he who has placed the statues of (*the gods*) in this palace, and has beautified Heliopolis, in like manner as he has honoured the Sun himself, the sovereign of heaven.  The offspring of the Sun, the King immortal, has performed a goodly work."

### *Verse the Third.*

" I, the Sun, the God and Lord of heaven, have bestowed strength and power over all things, on king Rhamestes : he whom Horus, the lover of truth, the Lord of the Seasons, and Hephaestus (*i.e.*, Vulcan), the father of the Gods, have chosen on account of his valour, is the all-gracious king, the offspring and beloved of the Sun."

### Towards the East.

### *Verse the First.*

" The great God from Heliopolis, celestial, Horus the Brave, the son of Heron, whom the Sun begot, and whom the Gods have honoured, he is the ruler of all the earth; he whom the Sun hath chosen is the king, valiant in battle.  Him Ammon loves ; and him the all-glittering has chosen his eternal king."

## OF THE SIRIADIC COLUMNS.

### FROM JOSEPHUS.

"All these (the sons of Seth), being naturally of a good disposition, lived happily in the land without apostatising, and free from any evils whatsoever : and they studiously turned their attention to the knowledge of the heavenly bodies and their configurations. And lest their science should at any time be lost among men, and what they had previously acquired should perish, (inasmuch as Adam had acquainted them that a universal *aphanism*, or destruction of all things, would take place alternately by the force of fire and the overwhelming powers of water), they erected two columns, the one of brick and the other of stone, and engraved upon each of them their discoveries ; so that, in case the brick pillar should be dissolved by the waters, the stone one might survive to teach men the things engraved upon it, and at the same time inform them that a brick one had formerly been also erected by them. It remains even to the present day in the land of Siriad."[1]—*Extracted from Josephus' "Antiquities of the Jews,"* Book i. ch. 2.

NOTE BY THE EDITOR.—" We do not here propose to renew the inquiry concerning the celebrated antediluvian columns, or stelæ, on which the lore of

---

[1] Various readings of this word are given, as *Syriada*, *Sirida*, *Sciria*. Voss proposes that we should read, *Eirath*.

this primæval world, with all its wisdom, was said to be transmitted. Plato, it is well-known, speaks of these columns in the opening of the *Timæus.* We shall examine, in the 5th book, whether this be anything more than a figurative description, and how far we may be justified in assuming any connection between the Egyptian legend and the two pillars of Seth mentioned by Josephus. (*Antiq.* i., ch. 2). These pillars, it is obvious, have reference to the book of Enoch*; perhaps also to the pillars of Akikarus, or Akicharus, the Prophet of Babylon, (*or* the Bosphorus), whose wisdom Democritus is said to have stolen, and on which Theophrastus composed a treatise. In the Egyptian traditions that have come down to us, these primæval stelæ do not make their appearance until the third and fourth centuries. They are first mentioned in the so-called *Fragments of Hermes,* in Stobæus; afterwards, in Zosimus of Panopolis, evidently in the colouring of Judaising-Christian writers ; but, in their worst shape, in the fourth century, in the work of an impostor who assumed the name of Manetho. That in this latter instance, at least, they were connected with the narrative of Josephus, is shown by their allusion to the 'Syriadic Country.'"—Extracted from Bunsen's *Egypt's Place in History,* vol. i., p. 7, 8.

---

* See the English translation of this book from the Ethiopic by Abp. Lawrence, (Oxford, 1821), and compare with it the extracts from it in Syncellus, upon the so-called *Egregors,* alluded to in the Epistle of Jude (verse 6).

THE

# INDIAN FRAGMENTS:

FROM

# MEGASTHENES.

# INDIAN FRAGMENTS.

## MEGASTHENES.

" MEGASTHENES also appears to be of this opinion, informing us that no reliance can be placed upon the ancient histories of the Indians. 'For,' says he, ' there never was an army sent forth by the Indians, nor did ever a foreign army invade and conquer that country, except the expeditions of Hercules and Dionysus, (Bacchus), and this (*invasion*) of the Macedonians. Yet, Sesostris the Egyptian, and Tearcon (Tirhakah) the Ethiopian, extended their conquests as far as Europe. But Navocodrosorus (Nebuchadnezzar), the most renowed (*monarch*) among the Chaldeans, exceeded Hercules, and carried his arms as far as the Pillars[1] (*of Hercules, i.e.*, the Strait of Gibraltar), to which also, it is said, Tearcon[2] arrived. But Navocodrosorus led his army from Spain to Thrace and Pontus. Idanthursus the Scythian, also overran all Asia as far

---

[1] There are on either side of the Strait two mountains, here called *pillars*, viz., Gebel Tarifa and Abyla.

[2] Tirhakah, king of Ethiopia.

as Egypt. But none of all these ever invaded India.'

Semiramis died before she commenced the undertaking. But the Persians sent the Hydracæ to collect a tribute from India ; but they never entered the country in a hostile manner, but only approached it when Cyrus led his expedition against the Massagetæ. Megasthenes, however, with some few others, gives credit to the narratives of the exploits of Hercules and Dionysus (Bacchus) : but all other historians, among whom may be reckoned Eratosthenes, set them down as incredible and fabulous, and of the same stamp with the achievements of the heroes among the Greeks."—*Extracted from Strabo,* Book xv. 686.


## OF THE CASTES OF INDIA.

" Megasthenes says, that the whole population of India is divided into seven castes ; among which that of the Philosophers is held in estimation as the first, notwithstanding their number is the smallest. The people when they sacrifice and prepare the feasts of the dead in private, each makes use of the services of one of them. But the kings publicly gather them together in an assembly which is called the great Synod, at which, in the commencement of each new year, all the philosophers assemble at the gate (court) of the king, so that, whatever each of them may have collected of things useful, or may have observed relative to the increase of the fruits and animals, and of the state, he may produce it in public. And it is a law that if any one of them be three times convicted of falsehood, he shall be doomed to silence during life; but the upright they exonerate from tax and tribute. The second division is the caste of the Agriculturists, who are the most numerous and worthy. They pursue their occupation free from military duties and fear; neither concerning themselves with civil, nor public, nor indeed any other business. It often happens that at the same time and place the military class is arrayed and engaged with an enemy whilst the agricultural, depending upon the other, (*i.e., the military caste*) for protection, plough and dig without any kind of danger. And, since the land is all held of the king, they cultivate upon hire, paying rent of one-fourth of the produce. The third caste is that of the Shepherds and Hunters, to whom alone it is lawful to hunt, graze, and sell cattle, for which they give a premium and stipend. For ridding the land also, of wild beasts and birds which destroy the grain, they are entitled to a portion of corn from the king, and lead a wandering life, living in tents. After the Hunters and Shepherds, the fourth caste is that of the Artisans and Innkeepers, and bodily Labourers of all kinds, of whom some bring tribute, or, instead of it, perform stated service on the public works. But the manufacturers of arms and builders of ships are entitled to pay and sustenance from the king, for they work only for him.   The keeper of the military stores gives out the arms to the soldiers, and the governor of the ships lets them out for hire to the sailors and merchants.   The fifth caste is the Military, who, when disengaged, spend the rest of their time at ease, in stations or barracks assigned them by the king, so that, whenever occasion may require, they may be ready to march forth directly, carrying with them nothing else than their bodies.   The sixth caste consists of the Inspectors, whose business it is to pry into all matters that are carried on, and report them privately to the king, for which purpose in the towns they employ courtesans, and camp-followers in the camp.   They are chosen from the most upright and honourable men.   The seventh caste includes the Councillors and Assessors of the king, by whom the government, and laws, and administration are conducted. ∨ It is unlawful either to contract marriages with another caste, or to change one profession or occupation for another, or for one man to undertake more than one (*profession*), unless the person so doing shall be one of the Philosophers, who are privileged on account of their dignity.

As regards the Governors, some preside over the rural affairs, others over the civil, others, again, over the military.   To the first class is entrusted the inspection of the rivers, and the measurement of the fields after the inundations, as in Egypt, and the

covered aqueducts, by which the water is distributed into channels for the equal supply of all,
according to their wants. The same have the
care of the Hunters, with the power of dispensing
rewards and punishments according to their deserts. They collect also the tribute, and inspect
all the arts which are exercised upon the land,
as of wrights, (ὑλοτόμων), and carpenters, and the
workers of brass and other metals. They also construct the highways, and at every ten stadia they
place a mile-stone (στήλη), to point out the turnings
and distances. The governors of cities are divided
into six pentads, some of whom overlook the opera-
tive works, and others have charge of all foreigners,
distributing to them an allowance, and taking cogni-
zance of their lives, if they give them habitations ;
else they send them away, and take care of the goods
of such as happen to die, or are unwell, and bury
them when dead. The third class of (*governors*) take
registers of the births and deaths, and how and when
they take place ; and this (*is done*) for the sake of the
tribute, that no births, either of good or bad, nor any
deaths may be unnoticed. The fourth class has the care
of the innkeepers and exchanges : these have charge
also of the measures and qualities of the goods, that
they may be sold according to the proper stamps.
Nor is any one permitted to barter more unless he
pay a double tribute. The fifth class presides over
the manufactured articles, arranging them, and sepa-

rating the stamped goods from the common, and the old from the new, and laying a fine upon those who mix them.  The sixth and last class exact the tithe of all things sold, with the power of inflicting death on all such as cheat.  Each, therefore, has his private duties.  But it is the public business of them all to control the private, as well as civil, affairs of the nation, and to inspect the repairs of the public works, and prices, and the markets, and the ports, and temples.

After the civil-governors there is a third college, which presides over military affairs, and this, in like manner, is divided into six pentads, of which the first is consociated with the governor of the fleet; the second with him who presides over the yokes of oxen by which the instruments are conveyed, and the food for themselves and the oxen, and all the other baggage of the army.  They have with them, moreover, attendants who play upon drums and bells, together with grooms and smiths, and their under workmen ; and they send forth their foragers to the sound of bells, recompensing their speed with honour or punishment, and attending to their safety.  The third class have the charge of the infantry; the fourth of the cavalry ; the fifth of the chariots ; the sixth of the elephants.  Moreover, there are royal stables for the horses and beasts ; and a royal arsenal, in which the soldier deposits his accoutrements when he has done with them, and gives up his horse to the master of the horse, and the same with respect to his beasts. They ride without bridles; the oxen draw the chariots along the roads, while the horses are led in halters, that their legs may not be injured, nor their spirit impaired by the draught of the chariots. In addition to the charioteer, each chariot contains two riders; but, in the equipment of an elephant, its conductor is the fourth, there being three bowmen also upon it.

The Indians are frugal in their diet, more particularly in the camp; and, as they use no superfluities, they generally attire themselves with elegance.

*The relation of Strabo is continued, with an account of the laws and customs of the Indians, containing some extracts from Megasthenes irrelevant to the antiquities.*

## OF THE PHILOSOPHERS.

" That is much more worthy of credit which Megasthenes reports, that the rivers roll down crystals of gold; and that a tribute is collected from thence for the king, for this also takes place in Iberia (Spain). And, speaking of the Philosophers, he says that those who inhabit the mountains are votaries of Dionysus (Bacchus), and they point to traces of him among them, inasmuch as with them alone the vine grows naturally wild, as well as the ivy, and laurel, and myrtle, and the box, and other species of evergreens, of which, beyond the Euphrates there are none,

except such as are kept as rarities in gardens, and
preserved with great care. The following are also
customs of Dionysiac, (*or* Bacchic) origin, viz., the
wearing of linen tunics and turbans, the use of oils
and perfumes, and the preceding their kings with
bells and drums when he goes forth on a journey.
The inhabitants of the plain, however, are devoted to
the worship of Hercules."—*Extracted from Strabo*,
Book xv. 711.

## Of the Philosophical Sects.

" He makes also another division of the Philosophers, saying that there are two races of them, one of
which he calls the Brahmans, and the other the Germanes. Of these the Brahmans are the more excellent,
inasmuch as their discipline is preferable ; for, as soon
as they are conceived, they are committed to the charge
of men skilled in magic arts, who approach under the
pretence of singing incantations for the well-doing
both of the mother and the child, though, in reality,
to give certain wise directions and admonitions ; and
the mothers, who willingly pay attention to them, are
supposed to be more fortunate in parturition.

After their birth, they pass from the care of one
master to that of another, as their increasing age re-
quires the more superior. The Philosophers pass
their time in a grove of moderate circumference,
which lies in front of the city, living frugally, and lying

upon couches of leaves and skins. They abstain also from animal food, and intercourse with females, intent upon serious discourses, and communicating them to such as wish. But it is considered improper for the auditor either to speak, or to exhibit any other sign of impatience ; for, in case he should, he is cast out of the assembly for that day as one incontinent. After passing thirty-seven years in this manner, they betake themselves to their own professions, where they live more freely and unrestrained : they then assume the linen tunic, and wear gold in moderation upon their hands, and in their ears. They also eat flesh, except that of animals which are serviceable to mankind ; but they, nevertheless, abstain from acids and condiments. They practise polygamy for the sake of having large families, because they think that from many wives a larger progeny will proceed. If they have no servants, their place is supplied by the service of their own children ; for, the more nearly any person is related to another, the more is he bound to attend to his wants. The Brahmans do not permit their wives to attend their philosophical lectures, lest, if they should be imprudent, they might divulge any of their secret doctrines to the uniniti-ated ; and, if they be of a serious turn of mind, lest they should desert them. For, no one who despises pleasure and pain, even to the contempt of life and death, (as a person of such sentiments as they pro-fess ought to be), would voluntarily submit to be under the domination of another. They hold various opinions upon the nature of death ; for they regard the present life merely as the conception of persons presently to be born; and death they consider as the birth into a life of reality and happiness, to those who philosophise rightly. Upon this account they are studiously careful in preparing for death. They hold that there is neither good nor evil in the accidents which take place among men ; nor would men, they say, if they regarded them aright, (as mere visionary delusions), either grieve or rejoice at them. They, therefore, neither distress themselves, nor exhibit any signs of joy at their occurrence.

Their speculations upon nature, he says, are in some respects, childish, though he admits that they are better philosophers in their deeds than in their words; inasmuch as they believe many things contained in their mythologies. However, they hold several of the same doctrines which are current among the Greeks ; such as, that the world is generated and destructible, and of a spherical figure, and, that the God who administers and forms it, pervades it throughout its whole extent ; that the principles of all things are different, that water, for instance, is the first principle of the fabrication of the world; that after the four elements, there is a certain fifth nature, of which the heavens and stars are composed; that the earth is situated in the centre of the whole. They add much, of a like nature, concerning generation and the soul. They have also conceived many fanciful speculations, after the manner of Plato ; in which they maintain the immortality of the soul, and the judgments of Hades, (hell), and doctrines of a similar description. Such is Megasthenes's account of the Brahmans.

Of the Germanes, he says, those are considered the most honourable who are called Hylobii, and live in the woods upon leaves and wild fruits, clothing themselves with the bark of trees, and abstaining from sexual intercourse, and wine. They hold communication, by messengers, with the kings, who inquire of them concerning the causes of things ; and, by their means, the kings serve and worship the deity.

After the Hylobii, the second in estimation are the Physicians, philosophers who are conversant with men, simple in their habits, but not exposing themselves to a life abroad, living upon rice and grain, which every one to whom they apply freely gives them, and receives them into his house. They are able, by the use of medicines, to render women fruitful and productive, either of males or females ; but they perform their cures, rather by attention to diet, than by the use of medicines. Among medicines they approve more commonly of ointments and poultices : all others they consider not free from deleterious effects. These, and others of this sect, so exercise their patience in labours and trials, as to have attained the capability of standing in one position, unmoved, for a whole day. There are others also, who pretend to divination and enchantments, and are skilful in the concerns of the inhabitants, and of their laws. These lead a mendicant life among the villages and towns ; but the better class settle in the cities. They do not reject such of the mythological stories concerning Hades as appear to them favourable to virtue and piety. Women, among some of these sects, are suffered to philosophise, but, in that case, they are required to abstain from sexual intercourse."—*Extracted from Strabo*, Book v. p. 712.

## Of the Indian Suicides.

Megasthenes, in his account of the Philosophers, says, "There is no prescribed rule for putting an end to themselves ; but those who do it are esteemed rash. Those who are hardy by nature cast themselves upon a sword, or from a precipice : those who are incapable of labour leap into the sea ; those who are patient of hardships are strangled, while those of a fiery temperament are thrust into the fire. This last was indeed the fate of Calanus, an intemperate man, and addicted to the pleasures of the table, at the court of Alexander (*the Great*)."—*Extracted from Strabo*, Book xv. p. 718.

*End of the Indian Fragments of Megasthenes.*

## OF THE PHILOSOPHERS. FROM CLITARCHUS.

"According to the statement of Clitarchus, they place in opposition to the Brahmans, the Pramnæ, a contentious and argumentative set of men, who deride the Brahmans as arrogant, and ridiculous, on account of their studies in physiology and astronomy. They are divided into the Mountaineer, the Naked, the Citizen, and the Rural sects."

## OF THE INDIAN ASTRONOMY.
### FROM THE PASCHAL CHRONICLE.

"About the time of the construction of the Tower, (*i.e.*, of Babel), a certain Indian, of the race of Arphaxad, made his appearance; a wise man, and an astronomer, whose name was Andubarius. It was he who first instructed the Indians in the science of Astronomy."—p. 36.

---

NOTE BY THE EDITOR.—Although from the earliest times to which historical research carries us back, an active trade seems to have been carried on between India and Western Asia, yet, Megasthenes is the earliest authority to which we can appeal for information, regarding the immense continent lying between the Indus and the Ganges. In the Hebrew Scriptures, the ivory, apes, and peacocks, brought to Judea by the ships of Tarshish, are designated by genuine Hindu, (*i.e.* Tamil), names; [see my article, *Dravidian Languages* in the *English Cyclopæd.*), Supplement, *Arts and Sciences*]; and at least one city of Syria, (the Hierapolis of the Greeks), was called by the Sanskrit name of MABUG, from *maha* = great and *bága* = a god—while India is enumerated among the 127 provinces subject to the rule of Xerxes in Esther i. 1, and viii. 9. The Sanskrit, the ancient language of Hindustan, abounds in works of science, theology, law, grammar, and poetry—both lyrical and dramatic; yet, it is a remarkable fact, that no historical work exists in any language of India of a date anterior to the Mohammedan conquest, by Mahmood of Ghuzni, (A.D. 1,000), except the poetic chronicle of Kashmir, called the *Raja Tarangini*, and the Ceylonese historical work called the *Mâhawânso*. "That no Hindu nation but the Kashmirians," says Sir William Jones, "have left us regular histories in their ancient language we must ever lament"; while Monier Williams, the Sanskrit Professor at Oxford, says, (*Introd. to Nala*, p. xvii.), "all Hindu Chronology is more or less conjectural." It is, indeed, uncertain, at what period the Hindus acquired the art of writing; for "no inscriptions," says Professor Max Müller, (*Sanskrit Grammar*, p. 3), "have been met with in India anterior to the rise of Buddhism. The earliest authentic specimens of writing are the inscriptions of *Priyadarsi*, or *Asoka*, about B.C. 250. These are written in two different alphabets. The alphabet which is found in the inscription of Kapurdigiri . . . . is clearly of Semitic origin, and most closely connected with the Aramaic branch of the old Semitic, or Phoenician, alphabet . . . . while that which is found in the inscription of Girnar, and which is the real source of all other Indian alphabets, has not, as yet, been traced back in a satisfactory manner, to any Semitic prototype." It is therefore to the fortunate circumstance of Megasthenes,—who had accompanied Alexander the Great in his Indian Expedition—being accredited as Ambassador from Seleucus Nicator to Sandracottus, (whom we identify with the Chandragupta of Hindu story)—that we are indebted for the earliest information in regard to India which has reached western nations. The royal seat of this monarch was at PATA-LIPUTRA, (Palibothra, or Patna); and a poem by SOMADEVA, after relating the story of the revolution which took place at Pataliputra, and the massacre of Nanda, and his sons, speaks of the usurpation of Chandragupta, and of his residence there. The age of the great ASOKA—the third or fourth in direct descent from Chandragupta, is one of the well-known epochs of the promulgation of the Buddhist faith; for Mihindá, Asoka's brother, preached the doctrines of Buddha to the distant inhabitants of Ceylon. "The history of ancient India," says a writer in the *Quarterly Review* for July, 1870, "is like a series of writings on a palimpsest; behind Buddhism, which is our first historical starting point, we find a form of Hinduism, which is the last stage of the religion of the Brâhmanas, before it assumed its modern developments as we trace them in classical Sanskrit literature; and it is far behind the oldest of the Brâhmanas, that we must look for the period of the Rig-Veda, upon which all Sanskrit literature is based."

THE

# ATLANTIC AND PANCHAEAN
# FRAGMENTS:

FROM

## MARCELLUS AND EUEMERUS.

# ATLANTIC AND PANCHAEAN

# FRAGMENTS.

## Of the Atlantic Island.

### From Marcellus.

" That such and so great an island formerly existed,
is recorded by some of the historians who have
treated of the concerns of the outward sea. For
they say, that in their times there were seven islands
situated in that sea, which were sacred to Proserpine, (Persephone), and three others of an immense
magnitude, one of which was consecrated to Pluto,
another to Ammon, and the one which was situated
between them to Poseidon[1]; the size of this last island
was no less than a thousand stadia. The inhabitants
of this island preserved a tradition, handed down from
their ancestors, concerning the existence of the
Atlantic island, of prodigious magñitude, which had
really existed in those seas, and which, during a long
period of time, governed all the islands in the Atlantic Ocean. Such is the statement of Marcellus in his
" Ethiopian History."—*Extracted from Proclus in
Timæus.*

---

[1] *i.e.,* Neptune.

## PANCHAEAN FRAGMENTS.

### FROM EUEMERUS.[1]

" Euemerus, (the historian), was a favourite of Cassander the king, and being, upon that account constrained by his master to undertake some useful, as well as extensive, voyage of discovery, he says that he travelled southwards to the ocean, and having sailed from Arabia Felix, stood out to sea several days, and continued his course among the islands of that sea, one of which far exceeded the rest in magnitude, and this island was called Panchæa.

He observes, that the Panchæans who inhabited it were singular for their piety, honouring the gods with magnificent sacrifices, and superb offerings of silver and gold.   He says, moreover, that the island was consecrated to the gods, and mentions several other remarkable circumstances relative to its antiquity, and the richness of the arts displayed in its institutions and services, some of which we have related in the books preceding this.  He relates also, that upon the brow of a certain very high mountain in it, there was a temple of the Triphylaean Zeus, founded by him at the time he ruled over all the

---

[1]   Or Euhemerus of Messana, an atheistic philosopher, friend of Cassander, king of Macedon.

habitable world, whilst he was yet resident amongst
men. In this temple stood a golden column, on
which was inscribed, in the Panchaean characters, a
regular history of the actions of Ouranos, and Kronus,
(Saturn), and Zeus (Jupiter).

In a subsequent part of his work, he relates that
the first king was Ouranos, a man renowned for
justice and benevolence, and well conversant with
the motion of the stars; and, that he was the first
who honoured the heavenly Gods with sacrifices,
upon which account he was called Ouranos (Heaven).
He had two sons by his wife Hestia, (Vesta), who
were called Pan and Kronus; and daughters Rhea[1]
and Demetra.[2] And Kronus reigned after Ouranos;
and he married Rhea, and had by her Zeus, and Hera,[3]
and Poseidon. And when Zeus succeeded to the
kingdom of Kronus he married Hera, and Demetra,
and Themis, by whom he had children; by the first,
the Curetes[4]; and Persephone, (Proserpine), by the
second, and Athena, (Minerva), by the third. He
went to Babylon, where he was hospitably received
by Belus, and afterwards passed over to the island of
Panchæa, which lies in the ocean, where he erected

---

[1] Cybele, "the great mother," the Ops of the Roman
mythology.

[2] Ceres.

[3] Juno.

[4] Priests of Jupiter in the island of Crete, and of the
goddess Cybĕlĕ.

an altar to Ouranos, (Heaven), his forefather.   From
thence he went into Syria to Cassius, who was then
the ruler of that country, from whom Mount Casius,[1]
(*on the borders of Egypt*), receives its name.   Passing
thence into Cilicia, he conquered Cilix, the governor
of those parts ; and, having travelled through many
other nations, he was honoured by all and universally
acknowledged as a god."—*Eusebius Præp. Evang.* ii.,
*as quoted from Diodorus Siculus Ecl.*, p. 681.

---

[1] Casius is the name of a mountain on the coast of
Egypt, now called *Ras Kasaroun.*   It lies east of Pelusium.
Another Mount Casius, *(Jebel Okrah)*, is placed in the
north of Syria, on the coast, south of the Orontes.   It is
uncertain which Mount Casius is intended in the text.

*End of the Atlantic and Panchæan Fragments.*

# MISCELLANEOUS FRAGMENTS.

# MISCELLANEOUS FRAGMENTS.

## HECATAEUS OF ABDERA.

" For Hecataeus of Abdera, who was both a philosopher, and one very useful in active life, was a contemporary of Alexander the Great in his youth, and was afterwards with Ptolemy, the son of Lagus. He wrote a book expressly about the Jewish affairs, (not by-the-by only), out of which book I am willing to run over a few things, of which I have been treating by way of epitome. And, in the first place, I will demonstrate the time when this Hecataeus lived. For he mentions the battle between Ptolemy and Demetrius, King of Syria, near Gaza, which was fought in the eleventh year after the death of Alexander the Great, and in the cxvii. Olympiad, as Castor relates in his history. For, when he had set down this Olympiad, he says further, that in this Olympiad, Ptolemy, the son of Lagus, conquered in battle at Gaza, this Demetrius, King of Syria, the son of Antigonus, who was surnamed Poliorcetes. Now it is agreed by all, that Alexander the Great died in the cxiv. Olympiad. It is, therefore, evident that our nation, (the Jews), flourished in his time, and in the time of Alexander the Great. Wherefore, Hecataeus

M

speaks to the same purpose as follows, viz., that
Ptolemy, after the battle at Gaza, got possession of
the places in Syria ; and many when they heard of
Ptolemy's moderation and humanity, went along with
him to Egypt, and were willing to assist him in his
affairs ; one of whom, says Hecataeus, was Hezekiah,
the high-priest of the Jews, a man of about sixty-six
years of age, and held in great dignity among his
own people (the Jews).    He was a very sensible
man, and could speak ably, and was very skilful in
the management of affairs, if any man ever were so,
although, as he says, all the priests of the Jews took
tithes of the products of the land, and managed public
affairs, and were in number not above 1,500 at the
most.    Hecataeus makes mention of this Hezekiah
a second time, and says, that as he was possessed of
so great a dignity, and was become familiar with us,
so did he take certain of those that were with him,
and explained to them all the circumstances of their
people, for he had all their habitations and civil
polity down in writing.    Moreover, Hecataeus de-
clares again, ' what regard we have for our laws, and
that we resolve to endure anything rather than trans-
gress them, because we think it right for us to do so.
Whereupon he adds, that although they are held in
bad reputation among their neighbours and among
all those who come to them, and have been often
treated reproachfully by the kings, and satraps of
Persia, yet they cannot be dissuaded from carrying

out what they think best; and when they are stripped
of everything on this account, and are tortured, and
brought to the most terrible kinds of death, they meet
them, (*i.e.*, the tortures), after a most extraordinary
manner, beyond all other people, and will not re-
nounce the religion of their forefathers. Hecataeus
also produces not a few incontestible proofs of this
their resolute tenaciousness of their laws, when he
informs us, that 'When once Alexander the Great
was at Babylon, and had purposed to rebuild the
temple of Belus, which had fallen to decay, and in
order thereto, he commanded all his soldiers in
general to carry earth thither, the Jews, and they
alone, would not comply with that command. Nay,
they underwent blows, and were mulcted in heavy
fines on this account, until the king forgave them, and
permitted them to live in quiet. He says, moreover,
that when the Macedonians came to them into that
country, and demolished the [old] temples, and the
altars, they assisted them in demolishing them all ;
but, (for not assisting them in rebuilding them), they
either underwent the payment of fine to the Satraps,
or, sometimes obtained forgiveness,' adding further,
that 'these men deserve to be admired on that
account.' He also speaks of the mighty populousness
of our, (the Jewish), nation, and says, that 'the Persians formerly carried away into captivity many ten
thousands of our people to Babylon, as also, that not
a few ten thousands were removed, after the death

of Alexander, into Egypt and Phoenicia, on account of the rebellion in Syria.' He also takes notice in his History how large the country is, which we inhabit, as well as of its excellent character, saying that 'the land which the Jews inhabit contains three millions of arourae, (or Egyptian acres), and is generally of a most excellent and fruitful soil ; nor is Judea of lesser dimensions.' The same writer describes our city of Jerusalem, as of a most excellent structure, and very large, and inhabited from the most ancient times. He also discourses of the number of men in it, and of the construction of our temple, after the following manner : 'There are many fortresses and villages,' says he, 'in the country of Judea ; but there is one fortified city, of about fifty furlongs in circumference, which is inhabited by 120,000 men, and this city they call Jerusalem. There is about the middle of the city a wall of stone, the length of which is 500 feet, and the breadth 100 cubits, with double cloisters (or having double gates). In the same place there is a square altar, not made of hewn stone, but composed of white stones gathered together, having each side twenty cubits in length, and ten cubits in height. Near it is a large edifice, wherein there is an altar, and a candlestick, both of gold, and two talents in weight. Upon these there is a light, which is never extinguished, neither by night nor by day. There is no image nor votive offering : nothing at all is there planted, neither a grove nor anything of the kind. Priests remain night and day in the temple, performing certain purifications, to whom it is altogether prohibited, while there, to drink wine. Hecataeus also testifies, that we, (the Jews), fought as auxiliaries in the army of Alexander, and afterwards in the service of his successors. I will add further what he learned, as he says, when he was himself with the same army, concerning what was done by a certain Jew in that expedition. He thus relates the story: 'As I was myself going to the Red Sea, there followed us a man, whose name was Mosollam : he was one of the Jewish horsemen who conducted us, a person of great courage, of a strong body, and one allowed by all to be the most skilful archer among either the Greeks or barbarians. Now, this man, as people were passing along the road in great numbers, and a certain augur was taking an augury by a bird, and required them all to stand still, Mosollam enquired what they were staying for. Hereupon the augur showed him the bird from whence he took his augury, and told him, that if the bird stayed where he was, they ought all to stand still; but, that if he got up and flew onward, they ought to advance ; but, on the other hand, if he flew backward, they must retire again. To this Mosollam made no reply, but, drawing his bow, shot at the bird, hit it, and killed it. When, therefore, the augur and others of the company were very angry, and cursed him, he answered them thus : 'Why are you so mad as to take this most wretched bird into your hands! How can this bird give us any true information concerning our march, which had not the foresight even to save himself? For, had he been able to foresee the future, he would not have come to this place, but would have been afraid, lest Mosollam the Jew should shoot at and kill him.'

But of the testimony of Hecataeus we have said enough; such as desire to know more of them may easily obtain them from his book."


FROM JOSEPHUS AGAINST APION, Book ii. sec. 4.

"For Alexander did not, therefore, assemble, or get together some of our nation to Alexandria, because he wanted inhabitants for this his city, on the building of which he had bestowed so much pains; but this was given to our people, (the Jews), for a reward, because he had, upon a careful trial, found them all to be men of virtue and fidelity to him. For, as Hecataeus says concerning us, 'Alexander honoured our nation, (the Jews), to such a degree that, for the equity and fidelity which the Jews manifested towards him, he permitted them to hold the country of Samaria free from tribute. Of the same opinion was Ptolemy, the son of Lagus, as to those Jews who dwelt in Alexandria.' For he entrusted the fortresses of Egypt into their hands, believing they would keep them faithfully, and valiantly; and, when he was

desirous of securing the government of Cyrene, and
the other cities of Libya to himself, he sent a body
of Jews to inhabit them."

---

## AGATHARCHIDES OF CNIDUS.

"I shall not think it too much for me to name
Agatharchides, as having made mention of us Jews,
though in the way of derision at our simplicity, as he
supposes it to be. For, when he was discoursing of
the affairs of Stratonice, 'how she came out of Mace-
donia into Syria, and left her husband, Demetrius,
while yet Seleucus would not marry her as she
expected, but while he was raising an army at
Babylon, stirred up a rebellion about Antioch, and
how, after the king had returned, and on his taking
Antioch she fled to Seleucia, and might have sailed
away immediately had she not complied with a dream
which forbade her to do so, and hence was captured
and put to death.'

When Agatharchides had premised this story, and
had jested upon Stratonice for her superstition, he
gives a like example of what was reported concerning
us, and writes thus : ' There are a people called Jews,
who dwell in a city, the strongest of all cities, which
city the inhabitants call Jerusalem. They are accus-

tomed to rest on every seventh day, at which times they make no use of their arms, nor meddle with husbandry, nor take care of any affairs of life, but spread out their hands in their holy places, and pray till the evening. Now it came to pass, that when Ptolemy, the son of Lagus, came against this city with his army, these men, in observing this mad custom of theirs, instead of guarding the city, suffered their country to submit itself to a bitter lord ; and their law was openly proved to have commanded a foolish practice. This accident taught all other men but the Jews, to disregard such dreams as these were, and not to follow the like idle suggestions, delivered as a law, when, in such uncertainty of human reasonings, they are at a loss what they should do.' Now this our procedure seems a ridiculous thing to Agatharchides ; but it will appear, to such as consider it without prejudice, a great thing, and one that deserved many encomiums ; I mean, when certain men constantly prefer the observation of their laws, and their religion towards God, before the preservation of themselves and their country."—*From Josephus against Apion*, Book i. sec. 22.

CONCERNING THE SEPTUAGINT VERSION, OR THE
TRANSLATION OF THE HEBREW BOOKS MADE
INTO GREEK BY ORDER OF PTOLEMY PHILA-
DELPHUS, KING OF EGYPT.

*From the Epistle of Demetrius Phalereus, keeper of
the Royal Library at Alexandria, to the king.*

DEMETRIUS TO THE GREAT KING.

"When thou, O king, gavest me a charge concerning the collection of books that were wanting to fill
your library and the care that ought to be taken
about such as are imperfect, I have used the utmost
diligence about those matters. And I hereby inform
you, that we want the books of the Jewish legislation,
with some others, for they are written in the Hebrew
characters, and, being in the language of that nation,
are to us unknown. Now it is necessary that thou
shouldst have accurate copies of them. And indeed,
this legislation, (the law of Moses), is full of hidden
wisdom, and entirely blameless, as being the legislation of God. For which cause it is, as Hecataeus
of Abdera says, that the poets and historians make
no mention of it, nor of those men who lead their
lives according to it, since it is a holy law, and ought
not to be published by profane mouths. If then it
please thee, O king, thou mayest write to the high

priest of the Jews, to send six of the elders out of every tribe, and those, such as are most skilful of the laws, that by their means we may learn the clear and consistent meaning of those books, and may obtain an accurate interpretation of their contents ; and so may have such a collection of these as may be suitable to thy desire."—*From Josephus's Antiquities of the Jews*, Book xii. section 4.

---

## HIEMPSAL.

### FROM SALLUST.

### *De Bello Jugurthæ.*

" But what race of men first had possession of Africa, and who afterwards arrived, and in what manner they have become blended with each other, though the following differs from the report which is commonly current, yet I will give it, as it was interpreted to me from the Punic, (*i.e.*, Carthaginian) books, which are called '*the books of King Hiempsal*.' ' The Gaetulians and Libyans,' says he, ' possessed Africa at first, a rough unpolished people, whose food, like that of cattle, consisted of the herb of the field, to which they added the flesh of wild animals. They were ruled neither by custom, law, nor any government; but strolling and wandering about, had their abode wherever night compelled them to stay. But after Hercules had perished in Spain, as the Africans suppose, his army, composed of men belonging to different nations, upon the loss of their leader, contending among themselves for the chief command, soon dwindled away. Of this numerous host the Medes, Persians, and Armenians, having been conveyed in ships to Africa, occupied those places nearest to the Mediterranean Sea. The Persians, however, settled nearer the (Atlantic) Ocean ; and, in place of houses, used their ships, turned bottom upwards, there being no wood in the country, nor any opportunity of buying, nor even of bartering with the Spaniards for any. Moreover, a wide sea and an unknown language prevented all intercourse. These colonists, by degrees mixed with the Gaetulians,[1] (*i.e., the aborigines*) in marriage. From the circumstance, however, of their frequently making trial of different soils, and the consequent shifting about from place to place, they called themselves *Numidians*.[2] And, to this day, the cottages of the Numidian

---

[1] The Gaetulians are the Berber tribes, now known by the names of Kabyles, Shelloofs, Beni-Mezab, &c., who are cognate in race and language with the aborigines of the Canary Islands. Their languages constitute the sub-Semitic branch of the Semitic linguistic family. Vide my article *Semitic Languages*, in the *English Cyclopædia*, Supplement (Arts and Sciences).

[2] From the Greek νεμειν, *to feed*, because they were fed, or maintained, by wandering about like grazing cattle.

peasants, which are called by them *mapalia*, are oblong, with their sides bulging out, like the hulls of ships. Now the Libyans joined the Medes and Armenians, for they lived nearer the African (*i.e.*, Mediterranean) Sea, the Gaetulians more under the sun, (*i.e.*, further south, not far from the scorching latitudes), and these, (*i.e.*, the Liby-Medians and Armenians) very soon had towns : for, divided from Spain only by the Strait (of Gibraltar), they and the Spaniards began to interchange commodities, (or barter) with one another. The Libyans, however, in course of time corrupted their name, calling them, in their barbarous language, Mauri, (or Moors), instead of Medi or Medes.

But the affairs of the Persians were soon in a flourishing condition, for afterwards, under the name of Numidians, (having separated from their parents on account of their vast numbers), they obtained possession of those parts nearest to Carthage, which are now called Numidia. Afterwards both parties, relying on one another, reduced their neighbours to subjection, either by arms or terror, and acquired for themselves, especially those who had advanced nearest to our, (*i.e.*, the Mediterranean) Sea, both glory and reputation ; the Libyans being less warlike than the Gaetulians. Finally, most of the lower parts, (*i.e.*, the north coast), of Africa were seized upon by the Numidians, all the conquered tribes being confounded in the name and nation of their rulers. In subse-

quent times the Phœnicians, some with the object of
diminishing the overflowing population at home,
others through a longing for power, having gained
over the people, together with those fond of changes
in government, to their undertaking, built Hippo,[1]
Hadrumetum, and Leptis, with other towns on the
coast. These cities, having grown much larger in a
short time, became some a security, others an orna-
ment to their founders. As to Carthage[2] itself, I

---

[1] There are two ancient cities on the north coast of Africa
which were formerly called Hippo (Phœnician עֻבּוֹ UBBO,
*a bay*). The one was Hippo Regius, once the residence of
the Numidian kings, and the episcopal see of St. Augustine,
now Bona. It is between the Cap de Fer (Ras Hadeed)
and La Calle ; the other, formerly called Hippo Zarytus
(*i.e.*, Hippo of the Canal) standing on a beautiful land-
locked harbour, with a narrow entrance (like a canal) to the
Mediterranean,· is now called Ben Zert (*i.e.*, son of the
canal). The former is in Algeria, and belongs to the
French ; the latter to Tunis. It is uncertain which of the
two is intended by our author.

[2] Carthage was founded by Dido, who is also called
Elisa, about 100 years before Rome. Upon the murder
of her husband, (Sichæus or Acerbas), by Pygmalion her
brother, she fled from Tyre, and founded this famous city.
It was for many centuries the rival of Rome, but about
150 B.C. it was destroyed by Scipio, the Roman general.
It is said to have continued burning for seventeen days.
Extensive ruins and mounds of earth, extending from the
sea to the walls of Tunis, along the shore of the lake, with
here and there a few broken arches of an aqueduct, are all
that remain of this once proud city, whose circumference,
it is said, was nearly twenty-four miles.

think it better to be silent, rather than say but little on such a subject, and besides, brevity obliges me to hasten to another."—*Extracted from Sallust de Bello Jugurthæ*, cap. xvii—xix.

---

## VELLEIUS PATERCULUS AND ÆMILIUS SURA.

" The Asiatic empire was subsequently transferred from the Assyrians, (who had held it 1,070 years), to the Medes, from this time for a period of 870 years. For Sardanapalus, King of the Assyrians, a man wallowing in luxury, being the thirty-third in succession from Ninus and Semiramis, the (*reputed*) founders of Babylon, from whom the kingdom had passed in a regular descent from father to son, was deprived of his empire, and put to death by Arbaces the Mede. . . . Æmilius Sura, also, in his *Annals of the Roman People*, says, That the Assyrian princes extended their empire over all nations. They were succeeded by the Medes, then by the Macedonians, and shortly afterwards by two kings, Philip and Antiochus, both of Macedonian origin, who, not long after the destruction of Carthage, were conquered by the Romans, who then obtained the empire of the world. To this time, from the beginning of the reign of Ninus, King of the Assyrians, who first obtained the empire, there has elapsed a period of 1,995 years."—*Extracted from the Roman History of Velleius Paterculus*, Book i. chap. 6.

---

## CLEANTHES.

Cleanthes was a Stoic philosopher, born at Assos, in the Troad, about B.C. 264. On his arrival at Athens he attended the lectures of Zeno, the Stoic, while so great was his poverty that, in order to maintain himself, he was obliged to draw water for the gardens of Athens by night, to provide himself the means of devoting himself to philosophy by day, whence he was nicknamed Phreantes, or the well-drawer. He was accustomed, from want of means to purchase writing materials, to write down on the blade-bones of oxen, and on pieces of pottery, his notes of the lectures delivered by Zeno, whose pupil he remained for nineteen years, and whom he succeeded in his school. Among his disciples were King Antigonus, and the philosopher Chrysippus. He is said to have taught that the sun is the ruling principle of the world. A specimen of his teaching has come down to us in his noble hymn to Jupiter, one of the most sublime efforts of poetry outside the canon of revelation :

## THE HYMN OF CLEANTHES.

### *Extracted from Stobæus.*

### TO JUPITER.

"O thou who, under several names, art adored, but whose power is entire and infinite ; O Jupiter, first of immortals, sovereign of nature, governor of all, and supreme legislator of all things, accept my suppliant prayer, for to man is given the right to invoke thee. Whatever lives and moves on this earth drew its being from thee ; we are a faint similitude of thy divinity.

I will address, then, my prayers to thee, and never will I cease to praise thy wondrous power. That universe suspended over our heads, and which seems to roll around the earth, obeys thee : it moves along, and silently submits to thy mandate. The thunder, minister of thy laws, rests under thy invincible hands ; flaming, gifted with an immortal life, it strikes, and all nature is terrified. Thou directest the universal spirit which animates all things, and lives in all beings.

Such, O almighty king, is thy unbounded sway ! In heaven, on earth, or in the floods below, there is nought performed or produced without thee, except

the evil, which springs from the heart of the wicked.
By thee confusion is changed into order : by thee
the warring elements are united.  By a happy agreement, thou so blendest good with evil, as to produce
a general and eternal harmony in all things.   But
man, wicked man, alone breaks this great harmony
of the world.   Wretched being, who seeks after
good, and yet perceives not the universal law which
points out the way to render him at once good and
happy.   He abandons the pursuit of virtue and
justice, and roves where each passion moves him.
Sordid wealth, fame, and sensual pleasures become,
by turns, the objects of his pursuit.   O God, from
whom all gifts descend, who sittest in thick darkness,
thunder-ruling Lord, dispel this ignorance from the
mind of man ; deign to enlighten his soul ; draw it to
that eternal reason which serves as thy guide and
support in the government of the world ; so that,
honoured with a portion of this light, we may, in our
turn, be able to honour thee, by celebrating thy great
works unceasingly in a hymn.   This is the proper
duty of man.   For surely nothing can be more de-
lightful to the inhabitants of the earth or the skies,
than to celebrate that divine reason which presides
over nature."—*From Rev. H. Card's Literary Recre-
ations*, 1811, p. 10.

## OF THE CHALDÆAN OBSERVATIONS

### FROM PLINY.

" Anticlides relates, that letters were invented in Egypt, by Menon, fifteen years before Phoroneus, the most ancient King of Greece, and he endeavours to prove it by the monuments.   On the other hand, Epigenēs, a writer of very great authority, informs us, that among the Babylonians, observations of the stars were preserved, inscribed upon baked tiles, extending to a period of 720 years.   Berosus and Kritodemus, who are the most moderate in their calculations, nevertheless extend the period of the observations to 480 years.   Whence may be inferred the eternal use of letters among them."—*Nat. Hist.* lib. vii., 56.

---

*For the following interesting extract I am indebted to* DR. SAMUEL BIRCH, *Keeper of Oriental Antiquities in the British Museum.*

### THE MANNERS OF THE BABYLONIANS.

#### FROM NICOLAS OF DAMASCUS.

" In the reign of Artæus, the King of the Medes, and one of the successors of Sardanapalus, King of the Assyrians, there was amongst the

Medes, one Parsondēs, a man renowned for his courage and strength, and greatly esteemed by the King, on account of his good sense, and the beauty of his person. He particularly excelled in the chase, and in battle, whether he fought on foot, from his chariot, or on horseback. Now this Parsondēs observed, that Nanarus, (the governor or tributary king), of Babylon, was very careful in his personal attire, and wore ear-rings, and shaved himself carefully, and was effeminate, and unwarlike, and he disliked him exceedingly ; so he asked Artæus, the King, to deprive Nanarus of his government, and to bestow it on himself. But Artæus, having bound himself by the compact entered into by Arbaces, was loth to act unjustly towards the Babylonian, and gave no answer to Parsondēs. The matter, however, reached the ears of Nanarus, who promised great rewards to any one of his sutlers who would catch his enemy. It happened one day that Parsondēs, when hunting, went far from the King, to a plain near Babylon. Sending his servants into a neighbouring wood, that they might drive out, by their shoutings, the wild beasts, he remained outside, to take the game. Whilst chasing a wild ass he separated himself from his attendants, and came to a part of the Babylonian territories, where the sutlers were preparing markets for Nanarus. Being thirsty, he asked of them to drink ; and they, delighted to have this opportunity of seizing him, gave him that

which he required, took charge of his horse, and bade
him refresh himself.   They then placed a sumptuous
feast before him, served him with very sweet wine,
mixed with a certain intoxicating drug, and brought
beautiful women to keep him company; so that, at
length, overcome by the wine, he fell fast asleep.
The sutlers then took him, and brought him bound
to Nanarus.   When Parsondēs had recovered from
the effects of the wine. Nanarus upbraided him for
his conduct.   'Why' said he, 'did you, who have
never suffered any wrong at my hands, call me a
man-woman (androgyne), and ask my government
of Artæus, as if I were of no account, although of
noble birth?   Many thanks to him that he did
not grant your request.'

Parsondēs, nothing abashed, replied, 'Because I
thought myself more worthy of the honour; for I
am more manly, and more useful to the king than
you, who are shaven, and have your eyes underlined
with stibium, and your face painted with white-lead.'
'Are you not ashamed, then,' said Nanarus, 'being
such as you describe yourself to be, to have been so
overcome by your stomach and passions, that you
should have fallen into the hands of one so greatly
inferior to yourself?   But I will quickly make you
softer and fairer than any woman.'   And he swore
by Belus, and by Mylitta—for such is the name
which the Babylonians give to their Venus; then
beckoning to a eunuch, 'Lead off' cried he, 'this

fellow. Shave, and rub with a pumice-stone, the whole of his body, except his head. Bathe him twice a day, and anoint him. Let him underline his eyes, and plait his hair as women do. Let him learn to sing, to play on the harp, and to accompany it with his voice, that he may be amongst the female musicians; with whom he shall pass his time, having a smooth skin, and wearing the same garments as they do. The eunuch did as he was commanded, and kept Parsondēs in the shade, washing him twice every day, and polishing him with a pumice stone, and making him pass his time in the same way as the women, so that he became, very shortly, fair, tender, and woman-like ; singing and playing even better than any of the female musicians. The King, Artæus, having offered a reward, and searched in vain for his favourite, at last concluded, that he had been devoured by wild beasts whilst hunting.

Parsondēs, having passed seven years in this mode of life at Babylon, induced a eunuch, who had been severely flogged, and insultingly treated by Nanarus, to run away, and inform Artæus of what had happened to him. Artæus immediately sent an envoy, to demand the liberation of his former favourite. But Nanarus, frightened, declared that he had never seen Parsondēs since he had disappeared. Artæus, however, sent a second ambassador, much greater in rank, and more powerful than the former one, and threatened by letter, to put to death the Babylonian, unless he delivered up his captive.

Nanarus, being now greatly alarmed, promised to give up the man, and, moreover, apologised to the ambassador, declaring, that he was sure the King would see, that he had justly treated one who had endeavoured to ruin him in the King's favour. He then entertained the ambassador with a great feast, during which entered, to the number of 150, the female players, amongst whom was Parsondēs. Some sang, and others played on the flute ; but the Mede excelled them all, both in skill and beauty, so that, when the feast was over, and Nanarus asked the ambassador, which of the women he thought superior to the rest in beauty, and accomplishments, he pointed, without hesitation, to Parsondēs. Nanarus, clapping his hands, laughed a long time, and then said, 'Do you wish to take her with you'? 'Certainly,' replied the ambassador. 'But I will not give her to you,' said Nanarus. 'Why then did you ask me?' exclaimed the ambassador. 'This,' said Nanarus, after a little hesitation, 'is Parsondēs, for whom you have come'; and, the ambassador disbelieving him, he swore to the truth of what he had said. On the following day, the Babylonian placed Parsondēs in a wagon, and sent him away, with the ambassador, to Artæus, who was at Susa. But the King did not recognise him, and was a long time before he would believe that so valiant a man could become a woman.

Parsondēs exacted a promise from Artæus that he would revenge him upon Nanarus. And when the King came to Babylon, he gave Nanarus ten days to do what was right; but the Babylonian, alarmed, fled to Mitraphernēs, the chief of the eunuchs, and promised him, for himself, ten talents of gold and ten gold cups, and 200 of silver, and 100 talents of silver money, and several suits of clothes; and for the King, 100 talents of gold, and 100 gold cups, and 300 of silver, and 1,000 talents of silver money, and numerous dresses, and other fine gifts, if he would save his life, and keep him in the government of Babylon. The eunuch, who was held in great estimation by the King, succeeded; but Parsondēs waited his opportunity, and afterwards, finding an occasion, took his revenge both on Nanarus and the eunuch."—Quoted in Layard's *Nineveh and its Remains*, vol. ii., p. 329—333, as translated by DR. BIRCH, from the *Prodromus Hellenikes Bibliothekes*, 8vo. *Paris*, 1805, p. 229.

---

## CANON OF THE KINGS OF EGYPT.

### FROM DIODORUS SICULUS.

" Some of them fable that gods and heroes first reigned over Egypt, during little less than 18,000 years, and that the last of the gods who reigned was

Horus, (the son of Isis). They relate, also, that the kingdom of Egypt was governed by men during nearly 15,000 years, down to the 180*th* Olympiad, in which we visited Egypt, that is during the reign of Ptolemy, called the younger Dionysus, (*i.e.*, Bacchus). The kings of Egypt were for the most part natives, except the Ethiopians, Persians, and Macedonians, who acquired the government for short periods. There reigned, altogether four Ethiopians, not in succession, but at intervals ; the length of whose reigns occupied collectively nearly 36 years. The Persians, under their king Cambyses, subdued the (*Egyptian*) nation, by force of arms and occupied the throne 135 years, inclusive of the period of the insurrections, which the Egyptians made from time to time, unable to endure the severity of their rule, and to submit to the impiety displayed by them towards the gods of the land. Lastly, the Macedonians and their successors reigned 276 years. All the rest of the time was filled up with native princes, viz., 470 kings, and 5 queens. After the gods, Menas (*i.e.*, Menēs), was the first king of the Egyptians. After him, it is said, that two of the descendants of the before-named king reigned during more than 1,400 years. Busiris. Then 8 of his descendants, of whom the last bore the same name as the first. He founded the city called by the Egyptians the city of the Sun, or Diospolis, but by the Greeks, Thebes. The 8th descendant of this king bore the surname of his father, Uchoreus, and built the city of Memphis, the most celebrated of all the cities of Egypt. Twelve generations of kings. Myris (or Mœris), who dug the lake above the city of Memphis. Seven generations of kings. Sesoōsis, whose exploits were the most celebrated, and the greatest of all the kings who preceded him, fitted out a fleet on the Red Sea, of 400 ships, and subdued all the islands, and all the parts of the mainland bordering on the sea as far as the Indies. He marched, also, with a mighty army by land, and subdued all Asia; passed over the Ganges, and conquered all India, even to the Ocean, and all the nations of the Scythians, and most of the islands of the Cyclades. He then invaded Europe, and overran all Thrace, and made it (*i.e.*, Thrace), the boundary of his military expeditions, and set up pillars (στηλας) in Thrace and many other places, commemorating his conquests. He also divided Egypt into 30 parts, which the Egyptians call *nomes*, and appointed governors (*nomarchs*) over each nome. And, after a reign of 33 years, he destroyed himself, on account of the failure of his eyesight.

Sesŏōsis, the second, the son of the preceding. Many kings succeeded him.

Amasis, who was conquered by Aktisanēs, the Ethiopian.

Aktisanēs, the Ethiopian.

Mendes, an Egyptian, who is the same as Marrhus.

He constructed the building called the Labyrinth, as a tomb for himself.

An interregnum for 5 generations.

Ketna (or Ketēs), who is Proteus.

Rhemphis.

Seven insignificant kings ruled, of whom no deed nor work worthy of record is handed down, except of one, who was called Nileus, from whom the river receives its name of Nilus[1], which formerly was called Ægyptus.

The 8th king was Chembres, the Memphite. He reigned 50 years and built the largest of the three Pyramids.

After his death, his brother, Kephrēn received the kingdom, and reigned 56 years. Some say, however, that it was not the brother, but the son of Chembres, who succeeded him, and that his name was Chabryïs.

Mykerinus, whom others call Cherinus, the son of the builder of the former Pyramid, undertook to build a third, but died before the completion of the work.

Tnephachthus.

Bocchoris (or Bonchoris), the wise, the son of Tnephachthus.

After a long time Sabacon reigned over Egypt, being by race an Ethiopian.

---

[1] In Arabic, NIL signifies *blue*, hence 'the blue Nile,' *Bahrat Neel.*

An interregnum of two years.

Twelve chiefs, 15 years.

Psammitichus the Saïte, who was one of the twelve chiefs.

After four generations reigned Apries, (Pharaoh Hophra), 22 years. He was strangled.

Amasis. He died after a reign of 55 years, at the time that Cambyses, king of Persia, invaded Egypt, *i.e.*, in the 3rd year of the 63rd Olympiad, in which (viz., the Olympic games) Parmenides the Camarinæan was victor."—*From* Diodorus Siculus, *Hist.*, Book ii.

FINIS.

# INDEX,

## RERUM ET VERBORUM.